Dover Memorial Library
Gardner-Webb University
P.O. Box 836
Bolling Springs, N.C. 28017

D0463388

In the Beginning . . .

Biblical Creation and Science

In the Beginning . . .

Biblical Creation and Science

by Nathan Aviezer

Professor of Physics
Bar-Ilan University

KTAV Publishing House, Inc, Hoboken N.J. 07030

BS
651
.A95
1990

Copyright ©1990
Nathan Aviezer

Library of Congress Cataloging-in-Publication Data

Aviezer, Nathan.
    In the beginning—: Biblical creation and science: by Nathan Aviezer.
        p.   cm.
    ISBN 0-88125-328-6
    1. Creation. 2. Bible. O.T. Genesis I—Criticism, interpretation, etc.
3. Bible and science. I. Title.
BS651.A95   1990
222'.1106—dc20   89–49127
                                                                         CIP

Manufactured in the United States of America.

First Printing	1990
Second Printing	1991
Third Printing	1992
Fourth Printing	1993
Fifth Printing	1995
Sixth Printing	1997

TO MY WIFE DVORA
COMPANION AND FRIEND FOR THIRTY YEARS

CONTENTS

FOREWORD

by

Professor Cyril Domb, FRS
formerly Clerk Maxwell Professor of Theoretical Physics
King's College, University of London

For the observant Jew, the words of the Torah represent eternal truths and are valid for all time. How should they be related to the general body of human knowledge? Throughout the centuries, this question has claimed the attention of Torah scholars, who made great efforts to familiarize themselves with current scientific knowledge. Where appropriate, they did not hesitate to use this knowledge to provide new interpretations of specific passages of the Torah. The present book by Professor Nathan Aviezer is a continuation of this tradition.

For the scientist, these are exciting times. Within the past few decades, a vast wealth of new scientific data has been amassed. Major technological breakthroughs—the transistor, the computer, the laser, and others—have made possible scientific measurements that could only have been dreamed of previously. The results of all this progress have been dramatic. There is hardly a field of science which has not been fundamentally altered by these new measurements. It is important to realize that until relatively recently, many scientific theories were based on not much more than educated guesswork and speculation.

But now the situation has been radically improved. Certain branches of science—cosmology, geology, molecular biology, and others—have, for the first time, been placed on a firm footing and buttressed by extensive experimental data. Hard facts have yielded new understanding, which has often led to quite unexpected results. Indeed, our view of the universe has been revolutionized. It is clearly time to ask: What are the implications of all these new scientific discoveries for one who believes in God? In the following pages, Professor Aviezer shows that the implications are profound.

That is what this book is all about. It is an attempt to correlate the most recent scientific data with the timeless passages of the Torah. The author has not hesitated to tackle the toughest challenge of all—the first chapter of the Book of Genesis. In analyzing these biblical verses, he demonstrates that passage after passage can be understood in terms of the latest scientific discoveries. Professor Aviezer has carried his investigations into every discipline that relates to the account of Creation given in Genesis, including cosmology, astronomy, geology, meteorology, biology, anthropology and archaeology. This distinguished scientist shows that in all these disciplines, current scientific evidence fits remarkably well with a literal interpretation of the text of Genesis. Moreover, he is able to give precise meaning in terms of modern scientific knowledge to a large number of phrases in the Genesis text that had previously been obscure and indefinite.

Professor Aviezer is well qualified to carry out this analysis. The author of nearly one hundred scientific publications, he was recently elected to Fellowship in the American Physical Society in recognition of his outstanding research contributions.

In this book, he tells us cogently and coherently of his findings. His references are to articles in prestigious scientific journals, most of them published within the present decade. He has shown in masterly fashion how they can throw light on difficult concepts and passages in the Creation narrative. In addition, at each stage, he focuses attention on physical features of the universe which from the secular point of view can only be regarded as a series of fortunate coincidences, but which for the religious believer are clear evidence of a grand design. Professor Aviezer does not pretend to have solved all the problems. But he has certainly provided fresh and thought-provoking insights which can contribute considerably to our understanding of this most challenging chapter of the Torah.

Following this analysis, it is natural to ask whether we are witnessing a convergence toward "ultimate" scientific theories. While I personally would not wish to hazard a prediction, an affirmative answer is consistent with the following passage from the Zohar, as amplified by the Vilna Gaon (for references, see H. Schimmel and A. Carmell eds., *Encounter*, pp. 199–200).

Commenting on the biblical phrase "the wellsprings of the great deep burst forth and the floodgates of the heavens were opened" (Genesis 7:11), the Zohar states that in the future, the gates of knowledge above ("the heavens") and the fountains of knowledge below ("the great deep") will be opened. The Vilna Gaon takes this passage to refer to the importance of science for the under- standing of Torah. He writes that "in order to understand and acquire the wisdom of the Torah, which is bound up with the light of the supreme wisdom, it is necessary to study also the seven wisdoms [branches of science] hidden in the lower world, the world of nature." He greatly encouraged his disciples to engage in scientific studies for this purpose.

Finally, it should be emphasized that this book does not abrogate the traditional freedom to interpret the biblical text figuratively when a literal interpretation gives rise to serious difficulties. (See, for example, Maimonides' Treatise on Resur- rection, translated by F. Rosner, Ktav, 1982, pp. 44–45). Profes- sor Aviezer himself has done so for the term "day," which he takes to mean a "phase" or a "period" in the development of the universe. There are good precedents for such an interpretation, as shown by the representative sample of the views of Torah scholars that it is reproduced in the book *Challenge*, a collection of essays on Torah and science, edited by Aryeh Carmell and myself. One must also bear in mind that the theory of relativity has radically changed our concept of the nature of time.

It is appropriate to end this foreword with a quotation from the greatest Torah scientist of all time. In a well-known respon- sum, Maimonides says the following of himself: "Before ever I was formed in the womb, the Torah knew me, and before I was born, she sanctified me—and handed me over to spread far and wide her fresh waters. The Torah is my beloved spouse, the wife of my youth, for with her love I was ravished at an early age. And yet, even she had many rivals—Moabites, Amorites, Sidon- ians, Edomites and Hittites. But God surely knows that these additional wives were taken only that they might act as perfu- mers, cooks, and housekeepers for her, and the better to display her beauty to the people and the princes—for she is extremely lovely to behold."

These striking words should give encouragement and gratification to Professor Aviezer who has also tried "the better to display her beauty to the people and the princes."

Cyril Domb

Department of Physics
Bar-Ilan University

PERSPECTIVES

In the analysis of the first chapter of the Book of Genesis, there has always been a certain reluctance to treat the text in its literal sense. Such reluctance is not surprising. Everyone with an awareness of science recognizes that there seem to be a large number of contradictions between the "facts" as represented by scientific knowledge and the "facts" implied by a literal reading of the first chapter of Genesis.

The question that is addressed in these pages is whether it is possible to understand the first chapter of Genesis as a record of events that actually occurred in the past. To answer this question, a detailed comparison is made between the biblical text and current scientific evidence. This analysis shows that, in contrast to the widespread misconception, there is in fact remarkable agreement between many biblical passages and recently discovered scientific facts in the fields of cosmology, astronomy, geology, meteorology, paleontology, anthropology, and archaeology.

As is well known, in all these areas of science, important and often dramatic progress has taken place in recent years. However, it is rarely appreciated to what extent this newfound knowledge can have a profound influence on our understanding of the first chapter of Genesis. Indeed, it is the thesis of this monograph that modern science has provided us with a unique opportunity to discover new and deeper insights into numerous biblical passages that otherwise seem enigmatic. Far from being the antagonist of the Book of Genesis, science has become an important tool for its understanding.[1]

A statement must be made at the outset about biblical chronology—the six days of creation. Any attempt to correlate the biblical text with scientific knowledge must necessarily understand the term "day" to mean a phase or a period in the development of the world, rather than a time interval of twenty-four hours. This idea is, of course, not new. The sages of the

Talmud long ago called attention to the fact that one cannot speak of a "day" or of "evening and morning" in the usual sense if there is neither sun nor moon in the sky. A careful discussion of the different viewpoints on the question of biblical chronology, as formulated by traditional Jewish commentators, has been given by Rabbi Eli Munk in his comprehensive etymological study of the first chapter of the Book of Genesis.[2] He concludes his analysis of biblical chronology with the following statement: "There is no consensus of traditional opinions about the definition of 'Day' in the Seven Days of the Beginning."[3] Munk emphasizes this divergence of opinion by printing the word "day" in italics throughout his book to avoid its being *misunderstood* as a time interval of twenty-four hours. The lack of consensus about biblical chronology is also apparent in the selection of quotations by traditional commentators presented in the book *Challenge.*[4]

The view adopted in the present book is that the six days of creation do not refer to a time interval of 144 hours, but rather to six specific phases in the development of the universe—from the initial creation to the appearance of man. This view is consistent with the position of many biblical commentators, ranging from the sages of the talmudic era down to the present century.[5]

The emphasis in the present analysis is on *events* and on statements of *fact* as they are recorded in the first chapter of the Book of Genesis. For these events and facts, we seek a counterpart in the scientific theory of the development of the universe. No pretense is made that everything has been explained. However, we will show that much of the biblical text *can* be understood in its literal sense on the basis of modern science.

Each chapter of this book is devoted to one of the days of creation. The chapter begins with the questions that one might ask about the biblical text. This is followed by an account of the relevant scientific background. We then give an interpretation of the biblical text based on scientific evidence. Each of these three elements requires some comment.

The questions that are raised are not the only ones that could be asked, nor is it implied that each question will seem compelling to every reader. These are the questions that are commonly asked—by some, in a sympathetic spirit of inquiry, whereas by others, as a provocative challenge to the biblical text. To each of these questions, modern science provides a new and illuminating explanation.

There is a tendency these days to disparage science by emphasizing the transitory nature of scientific theory. However, every competent scientist can distinguish between the more speculative theories and those that are firmly established. It is the former that are short-lived and whose demise is regularly reported in the popular press, whereas the latter have an excellent record for longevity. For example, the theory of relativity and the quantum theory have had unqualified success since their inception in explaining hundreds of different phenomena. Such well-established theories are constantly being refined and extended, but they do not undergo fundamental revision. Of course, the empirical nature of science precludes the possibility of absolute proof for any theory. However, the chance that a well-established theory will eventually be overthrown is extremely slight.

It will be shown that current scientific evidence provides an answer to each of the questions that is asked about the biblical text. This does *not* of course imply that the Book of Genesis should be read like a science textbook. But it is proposed that there exists a scientific explanation that is *consistent* with the text. Establishing this consistency is the task to which this book is dedicated.

NOTES

1. This point has been demonstrated in several recent works, such as the *Proceedings of the Association of Orthodox Jewish Scientists* and the important collection of essays edited by A. Carmell and C. Domb, *Challenge* (Jerusalem: Feldheim, 1978).

2. E. Munk, *The Seven Days of the Beginning* (Jerusalem: Feldheim, 1974).

3. Ibid., p. 50.

4. Carmell and Domb, pp. 124–140.

5. See ibid. and Munk, op. cit. Several of the more prominent Jewish commentators are cited in these pages. Further information about them, if desired, can be found by consulting any standard reference work, such as the *Encyclopaedia Judaica* or the *Encyclopaedia Britannica*.

The First Day
The Origin of the
Universe

GENESIS—CHAPTER 1

¹In the beginning, God created the heaven and the earth. ²Now the earth was desolate and chaotic, and darkness was upon the deep, and the spirit of God hovered over the water. ³And God said, "Let there be light," and there was light. ⁴And God saw that the light was good, and God separated the light from the darkness. ⁵And God called the light Day, and the darkness He called Night. And there was evening and there was morning—one day.

QUESTIONS

The events associated with the first day of creation are described in the opening five verses of the Book of Genesis. These verses contain several statements that seem incredible.

1. First and foremost, we read that God created the universe (1:1). The creation must surely be the most dramatic event that ever occurred. Why, then, cannot every scientist observe clear and undeniable evidence for the creation of the universe? Why are there, in fact, no signs *whatsoever* of the occurrence of such an event? Indeed, let us openly admit that the very concept of creation *ex nihilo* (i.e., something out of nothing) contradicts well-known laws of nature, such as the law of the conservation of mass and energy. This law of nature asserts that it is *impossible* to create something out of nothing.

2. We read that God created light (1:3). What light? The presently known sources of light include the sun and the stars, reflected light from the moon, and the light produced when one strikes a match or turns on a light switch. But on the first day, there was *no* sun, *no* stars, and *no* man. The nature of this light is thus a complete mystery that is never explained in any subsequent verse. Nevertheless, it was considered so important that the entire first day, one sixth of the story of creation, is devoted to this enigmatic light.

3. We read that God subsequently "separated" the light from the darkness (1:4). Darkness is not a *substance* that can be separated from light. The word "darkness" simply denotes the *absence* of light. If there is darkness, then there is no light; if there is light, then there is no darkness. Thus, there is no logical content to the notion of the separation of light from darkness.

4. We read that the universe began in a state of chaos (Hebrew *tohu va-vohu*) (1:2). No indication whatever is given in the text as to the nature of this chaos. Just what was chaotic? And how was the chaos removed, if indeed it was removed?

7

5. Finally, we read that the entire complex series of cosmological events necessarily involved in the creation of the universe occurred within a single day (1:5). It is well known that the duration of cosmological events is not measured in days or even in years, but in millions and billions of years.

These are some of the questions that one may ask. We shall now present the current scientific evidence that relates to each of the questions, assessing in detail the apparent contradictions between science and the Book of Genesis. It will be shown that, improbable as it may seem, scientific evidence discovered in recent years provides an explanation of the biblical text that is completely consistent with current scientific knowledge.

COSMOLOGY

Cosmology is the branch of science that deals with the origin and development of the universe. It is one of the oldest of the sciences, having been the subject of sustained interest for thousands of years in almost every civilization. However, until the present century, all cosmological studies were based on pure speculation, with little if any scientific basis. It is important to realize that the situation had not significantly improved even by the middle of the twentieth century. Professor Steven Weinberg, Nobel laureate from Harvard University, writes that "in the 1950s, the study of the early universe was widely regarded as not the sort of thing to which a respectable scientist would devote his time. . . . there simply had not existed an adequate observational and theoretical foundation on which to build a history of the early universe."[1]

The approach to cosmology that was fashionable in the 1950s was based on the idea that the universe we observe today has always existed and will always exist in essentially its present form.[2] Indeed, the assumed constancy of the universe is consistent with the results of thousands of years of continuous astronomical observation, which has produced a record of a fixed and unchanging sky, except for the apparent gradual rotation of the stars around the heavens as the earth revolves around the sun once each year. The pattern of stars and constellations that we see today is virtually identical to that recorded by the star-gazers of ancient civilizations. The tradition of stellar quiescence naturally suggests the idea of a constant universe and may have played a part in its acceptance—all without adequate scientific basis.

THE BIG-BANG THEORY

In 1946, George Gamow and his collaborators proposed an entirely different theory of cosmology.[3] The main features of this revolutionary theory are listed in the accompanying table, in which time is measured in billions of years. The present time is denoted by 15 because, according to the Gamow theory, *the universe began 15 billion years ago.* At that time, denoted by 0 in the table, there suddenly appeared *out of nothing* an enormous source of energy, called the primeval fireball but popularly known as the "big bang," hence the name "big-bang theory." The sudden appearance of the primeval fireball marked *the beginning of the universe* in the sense that before the big bang, nothing at all existed. Thus, the big bang is the precise realization of creation *ex nihilo.*

THE BIG-BANG THEORY

Event	Time (billions of years)
The present	15

Formation of atoms and molecules
Universe suddenly becomes
    transparent
Light begins shining and fills entire
    universe
	0.001

Sudden appearance of primeval fireball Beginning of the universe Big bang—creation *ex nihilo*	0

The term "fireball," commonly used by cosmologists, should not give the mistaken impression that something was actually burning. The fireball was an intense concentration of pure energy. A familiar example of concentrated pure energy is the bright spot of light that can be formed by focusing the sun's rays by means of a lens. To imagine the primeval fireball, one may think of a large ball of light that is many billions of times more intense than a focused spot of sunlight.

We put aside for the moment the all-important question of where the primeval fireball came from and proceed to describe some basic aspects of the theory. In particular, how did the primeval fireball develop into the universe as we know it? Our present universe is composed of matter (in the form of atoms and molecules), which is the basic constituent of everything we see, ranging from stars and galaxies to oceans and trees and animals. From where did all this matter come?

The answer is given by the famous formula of Einstein's theory of relativity

$$E = mc^2$$

where E denotes energy, m denotes matter, and c denotes the speed of light. This formula states that matter can be converted into energy. Moreover, because of the large value of c^2, a little bit of matter suffices to produce an enormous amount of energy. This matter-to-energy conversion is not merely a hypothetical possibility, but forms the basis for nuclear energy; its powerful bombs devastated Hiroshima and Nagasaki, but its peaceful use provides electric power for tens of millions of families. The big-bang theory utilizes the fact that Einstein's formula can work *both* ways; not only can matter be converted into energy, but energy can also be converted into matter. Although it requires a vast amount of energy to produce only a little matter, the amount of energy present in the primeval fireball was so enormous that it was the source of all the matter that now exists in the entire universe.

The form of energy present in the fireball was the energy of light, which is the same type of energy that the sun radiates. The term "light" is used here to denote a general phenomenon, called "electromagnetic radiation" by the scientist. This phenomenon is most easily explained by again referring to the sun. The sun emits electromagnetic radiation that the eye can see, called visible light. This light includes a spectrum of colors ranging from red to blue (the familiar colors of the rainbow). However, the sun also emits electromagnetic radiation that the human eye is incapable of seeing, called invisible light. The spectrum of "colors" of the sun's invisible light includes infrared radiation (which gives the skin the sensation of warmth), ultra-violet radiation (which causes the skin to tan), microwave radiation (used for cooking in microwave ovens), radio waves, X-rays, etc. There is *no* essential difference between the colors of visible light and those of invisible light; together they comprise the entire spectrum of electromagnetic radiation. A camera with appropriate film will record each of these colors equally well. Therefore, we follow the standard practice of using the term "light" to include *all* electromagnetic radiation, encompassing both visible and invisible light.

We now come to a most important event that occurred shortly after the big bang, at the time denoted by 0.001 in the table. In order to understand this event, some background information is necessary. The familiar form of matter is an atom, or a group of atoms called a molecule. However, when matter was initially formed, immediately after time zero, it did not exist in the form of atoms. The enormous temperature of the primeval fireball would have instantly disintegrated any atom. Therefore, matter existed in a different form called a "plasma". The important distinction between these two forms of matter is that an atom is electrically neutral, whereas a plasma consists of particles having either positive or negative electric charges. The properties of charged particles are such that a plasma "traps" light and prevents its free passage. For this reason, a plasma always appears dark to an outside observer.

Within a fraction of a second after the big bang, the universe consisted of the light of the primeval fireball interspersed with a plasma. Even though it was extremely intense, the light of the fireball was trapped by the plasma and could not "escape" to be "seen." To visualize this situation, imagine that the universe had been inhabited at that time by someone with a camera. The universe would have appeared *dark* to our cameraman because of the plasma, and any photographs taken would have resulted in pictures that were completely *black*, even though the universe was filled with the light of the fireball. It is as if one were to take photographs (without flash) in a totally dark room.

After time zero, the very hot primeval fireball cooled extremely rapidly. By the time 0.001 (see the table), it had cooled sufficiently to permit the charged particles of the plasma to combine and form atoms. The formation of atoms from the plasma was a vitally important event, being crucial for the universe to develop into its present form.

In contrast to a plasma, any region of space filled with free atoms and molecules is completely transparent. One need only think of our planet's transparent atmosphere, which is composed of molecules of air (mainly nitrogen and oxygen). Light shines freely through the atmosphere; from the surface of the earth, one clearly sees the sun, the moon, and the distant stars and galaxies. Therefore, when the plasma was suddenly transformed into atoms and molecules 15 billion years ago, the light of the fireball was no longer trapped by the plasma. Instead, the light began to "shine" visibly, and it soon filled the entire universe, as it still does to this very day.

This concludes our very brief description of the main features of the big-bang theory of George Gamow. As with any scientific theory, the criterion for acceptance is that the predictions of the theory must be confirmed. The most striking prediction of the big-bang theory is surely that the universe is filled with light, dating back 15 billion years to the very origins of time. This light, which is primarily in the invisible portion of the electromagnetic spectrum, has very special properties (which need not concern us here) that make it easily distinguishable from other sources of electromagnetic radiation. However, the predicted radiation had never been observed.

It is easy to explain why the predicted radiation was not observed. The primeval fireball was originally extremely hot and contained an enormous concentration of energy. However, with the passing of time, the fireball expanded and cooled, with the result that the radiant energy spread out. Today, after 15 billion years have passed, the energy of the fireball is very thinly spread and its electromagnetic radiation is so extremely weak that detecting it was technically impossible with the available scientific apparatus.

The situation regarding the big-bang theory can be summarized as follows. This theory of cosmology was completely different from generally accepted ideas. Indeed, the theory seems to border on the irrational. Moreover, for technical reasons, its dramatic prediction of the existence of a special radiation that fills the entire universe could not be tested. Therefore, it is not surprising that the big-bang theory was not taken seriously by the scientific community.

CONFIRMATION OF THE THEORY

In the years following the Second World War, major technological breakthroughs occurred in many fields. It was the era of the transistor, the laser, and the computer. Scientific instrumentation also underwent a radical improvement. Many experiments that were impossible to perform with the technology available in the 1940s became routine by the 1960s. Of particular relevance here, radiation detectors were also improved a hundredfold and more. In fact, by the 1960s, it had become technically feasible to detect the extremely weak electromagnetic radiation predicted by the big-bang theory.

In 1965, two American scientists, Arno Penzias and Robert Wilson of the Bell Telephone Research Laboratories, were using an extremely sensitive antenna to measure galactic radio waves. While testing their antenna, they observed some very weak unexpected electromagnetic radiation that seemed to be coming simultaneously from all directions in outer space. It was soon realized that this radiation was precisely what was predicted by the big-bang theory.

Since Penzias and Wilson first announced their findings, many other scientists have confirmed their measurements. At present, there is not the slightest doubt that this fundamental prediction of the big-bang theory has become a scientifically established fact. Moreover, other key predictions of the big-bang theory have also been confirmed. For example, the theory predicts that all the galaxies in the universe should be rushing away from each other at high speeds as a result of the initial explosion—the big bang. Moreover, the distant galaxies should move faster than the nearer ones. The predicted motion of the galaxies has been confirmed, primarily though the research work of the American astronomer Edwin Hubble, and the rate of the galactic motion is therefore called the Hubble constant. Another triumph for the big-bang theory relates to the chemical composition of the universe. The relative amounts of hydrogen and helium that are observed to be present in the universe are in excellent accord with the prediction of the theory.

Because of the confirmation of all its predictions, the big-bang theory has become *the accepted theory* of cosmology, with the abandonment of all competing theories. Today, scientists carry out research in cosmology *only* within the framework of the big-bang theory. The final mark of recognition of the validity of the big-bang theory occurred in 1978, when Arno Penzias and Robert Wilson were awarded the Nobel Prize in Physics for their fundamental discovery. Unfortunately, George Gamow could not share in this honor, because he died in 1968 and the rules of the Nobel Prize do not permit posthumous awards.

It would be difficult to overestimate the importance of the Penzias-Wilson discovery. Professor Steven Weinberg calls it "one of the most important scientific discoveries of the 20th century."[4] One can well understand the superlatives used by Weinberg. The big-bang theory has totally altered our conception of the origins of the universe.

THE BIBLICAL TEXT

It is now time to return to our initial program, a comparison between the biblical text and current scientific knowledge. Accordingly, we shall examine in detail each of the five points listed at the beginning of this chapter.

1. Creation

The creation of the universe has become an accepted scientific fact. The current scientific position regarding creation has been summarized by Professor P. A. M. Dirac, Nobel laureate from the University of Cambridge: "The development of radio-astronomy within the last few years has vastly increased our knowledge of distant parts of the universe. As a result, a violent beginning of the universe is now generally accepted."[5] Today, by making appropriate measurements, every scientist can see clear and unequivocal evidence supporting the view that creation indeed occurred.

It is instructive to quote a few statements made by the cosmologists who stand at the very head of their profession. Professor Stephen Hawking of the University of Cambridge writes: "The actual point of creation lies outside the scope of presently known laws of physics."[6] Professor Alan Guth of the Massachusetts Institute of Technology and Professor Paul Steinhardt of the University of Pennsylvania write: "The instant of creation remains unexplained."[7] Professor P. A. M. Dirac, Nobel laureate from the University of Cambridge, writes: "It seems certain that there was a definite time of creation."[8] The titles of two recent scientific books on cosmology are: *The Creation* by Professor Peter Atkins of the University of Oxford[9] and *The Left Hand of Creation* by Professor Joseph Silk of the University of California.[10] And finally, a recent scientific article published in one of the foremost international journals of physics carries the following title: "Creation of the Universe from Nothing."[11]

The term "creation" has clearly left the private preserve of the biblical scholar and has entered the lexicon of science. Indeed, there can no longer be any meaningful scientific discussion of cosmology without creation playing a leading role.

We now turn to the *central issue*—the vital question of what *caused* the sudden appearance of the primeval fireball that heralded the creation. In the words of some of the world's leading cosmologists, the creation of the universe is "outside the scope of presently known laws of physics"[12] and "remains unexplained."[13] In contrast to science, the Book of Genesis *does* give an explanation for what caused the creation of the universe—an explanation written in its very first verse: "In the beginning, God created . . ."

2. The Light

Cosmology has now established that the sudden unexplained appearance of the primeval fireball *is* the creation of the universe. The biblical passage "Let there be light" may therefore be understood as designating the creation of the primeval fireball— the big bang—that signals the creation of the universe. All the matter and energy that exists today throughout the universe results directly from this "light." Note in particular that there were not *two* separate, unconnected creations on the first day—the universe and the light—but only *one*.

3. Separation of Light

The big-bang theory explains that the universe originally consisted of a mixture of a plasma and the light of the primeval fireball. At that time, the universe appeared *dark* because of the plasma. The sudden transformation of the plasma into atoms shortly after the creation caused the electromagnetic radiation ("light") of the primeval fireball to "separate" from the previously dark universe and shine freely throughout space. This separation is called decoupling in scientific terminology.

The biblical passage "And God separated the light from the darkness" may be understood as referring to the decoupling of the light from the dark fireball-plasma mixture. This decoupled radiation ("light") was eventually detected 15 billion years later by Penzias and Wilson, earning them the Nobel Prize.

4. Chaos (Tohu va-Vohu)

Important developments have occurred in the big-bang theory since 1980 which fall under the general heading of the "inflationary universe," proposed by Guth and Steinhardt. A recent article summarizing these new findings contains the following words: "the universe began in a random chaotic state."[14] A recent book on cosmology discusses at length the phenomenon of the primordial chaos and its important cosmological implications.[15] This discussion appears in the section of the book called "Primeval Chaos," which is part of the chapter entitled "Chaos to Cosmos." Finally, Professor Andrei Linde of the Lebedev Physical Institute of Moscow has recently proposed the "chaotic inflation scenario" to describe the beginnings of the universe.[16] It lies beyond the scope of this monograph to explain the nature of this chaos and its importance, but it should be emphasized that the role of chaos in the development of the very early universe has become a major subject of cosmological research. The relevance of this to our discussion is clear: the Book of Genesis asserts that the universe began in a state of chaos (*tohu va-vohu*) (1:2).

5. Creation in a Single Day

It is a common fallacy to believe that because cosmological changes occur extremely slowly at the present time, it must have always been so. Indeed, this is precisely the philosophy behind the now-disproved earlier theories of cosmology. By contrast, according to the modern big-bang theory, a long series of dramatic cosmological changes occurred within an extremely short time at the very beginning of the universe. This point was brought home forcibly by Professor Steven Weinberg of Harvard University with his choice of a title for his popular book on modern cosmology: *The First Three Minutes*. It takes Professor Weinberg 151 pages of text and diagrams to describe the momentous cosmological changes that took place in our universe during a mere *three minutes*.

SUMMARY

A most appropriate summary to this chapter can be found in the words of Professors Guth and Steinhardt, who comment that "from a historical point of view, probably the most revolutionary aspect" of the modern theory of cosmology is the claim that matter and energy were literally created. They emphasize that "this claim stands in marked contrast to centuries of scientific tradition in which it was believed that something cannot come from nothing."[17]

In short, hundreds of years of intense scientific effort by some of the finest minds that ever lived has finally produced a picture of the origins of the universe that is in striking agreement with the simple words that appear in the opening passages of the Book of Genesis.

NOTES

1. S. Weinberg, *The First Three Minutes* (London: Andre Deutsch & Fontana, 1977), pp. 13–14.

2. H. Bondi, 1960, *Cosmology*, 2nd ed. (Cambridge: At the University Press, 1960).

3. Weinberg, loc. cit. G. T. Bath, *The State of the Universe* (Oxford: At the University Press, 1980), chap. 1.

4. Weinberg, p. 120.

5. P. A. M. Dirac, *Commentarii*, vol. 2, no. 11, 1972, p. 15.

6. S. W. Hawking and G. F. R. Ellis, *The Large Scale Structure of Space-Time* (Cambridge: At the University Press, 1973), p. 364.

7. A. H. Guth and P. J. Steinhardt, *Scientific American*, vol. 250, May 1984, p. 102.

8. P. A. M. Dirac, *Commentarii*, vol. 3, no. 24, 1972, p. 2.

9. P. W. Atkins, *The Creation* (Oxford: W. H. Freeman, 1981).

10. J. D. Barrow and J. Silk, *The Left Hand of Creation* (London: Heinemann, 1983).

11. A. Vilenkin, *Physics Letters*, vol. 117B, 1982, pp. 25–28.

12. Hawking and Ellis, p. 364.

13. Guth and Steinhardt, p. 102.

14. Ibid.

15. Barrow and Silk, op. cit.

16. A. Linde, *Physics Today*, vol. 40, September 1987, pp. 61–68. According to the proposal of "chaotic inflation," the universe we observe is embedded in a much larger structure, with the sudden appearance of the observable universe having been triggered by *chaos*. Professor Linde explains that immediately after its creation about 15 billion years ago, the observable universe was "subsequently describable by the usual big-bang theory" (p. 66).

17. Guth and Steinhardt, p. 102.

The Second Day
The Formation of the
Solar System

⁶*And God said, "Let there be a firmament in the midst of the waters, and let it separate waters from waters." ⁷And God made the firmament, and He separated the waters which were below the firmament from the waters which were above the firmament. And it was so. ⁸And God called the firmament Heaven. And there was evening and there was morning— a second day.*

QUESTIONS

The second day of creation deals with the formation of the heaven. The principal astronomical event that is described in Genesis 1:6–8 appears to be extremely improbable.

After being told that God made the firmament (i.e., heaven; "outer space" would be the modern term), we read that its function was to separate "the waters which were below the heaven from the waters which were above the heaven" (1:7). It is clear what is meant by "the waters which were below the heaven"; the phrase obviously refers to the oceans, the lakes, and the rivers. But what possible meaning can one attribute to "the waters which were above the heaven"? Is there any evidence at all for large bodies of water floating about in outer space? Indeed, the very idea borders on the irrational.

The preceding statement represents the popular view. We shall now present the recent astronomical data that relate to these questions, including the latest results obtained from the space program, which has greatly enhanced our understanding of the solar system. These recent findings provide an explanation of the biblical text that is consistent with current scientific evidence.

WATER IN OUTER SPACE

For those readers who find incredible the suggestion that outer space contains vast quantities of water (or ice), we quote the following account from the *Cambridge Atlas of Astronomy*, the authoritative, up-to-date encyclopedic reference work covering all aspects of planetary science:

In the morning of 30 June 1908, a fantastic explosion occurred in central Siberia. . . . Witnesses described an enormous meteoric bolide visible in the sky for a few seconds. Other witnesses at a distance of 60 kilometers from the point of impact were knocked over. . . . Seismic shocks were registered over the whole world. . . . The explanation now accepted is that this event was due to the collision with the Earth *of a block of ice weighing 30,000 tons* [emphasis added] which . . . released energy equivalent to that of a thermonuclear bomb of 12 megatons.[1]

A 12-megaton thermonuclear bomb has the same explosive power as *12 million tons of TNT.* Had this gigantic block of ice dropped from outer space to fall on, say, New York City or London, rather than in an uninhabited valley in central Siberia, a holocaust would have resulted.

Where did this enormous mass of ice come from? Is there more ice in outer space? And if so, where is it to be found?

Modern planetary research has shown that the outer regions of the solar system contain *vast quantities* of ice. One important source is the comets, with the cometary nucleus being essentially a gigantic ice cube. In fact, the 30,000-ton block of ice that fell from the sky in Siberia in 1908 was a very small piece of the nucleus of the comet Encke.[2] The currently accepted theory of comets was first proposed by Professor Fred Whipple of Harvard University, for many years the director of the Smithsonian Astrophysical Observatory.[3] The Whipple theory, now very well established, describes the comet as a "dirty snowball" because it is composed of ice interspersed with particles of dust and other interplanetary debris.

The numerical data relating to comets are guaranteed to stagger the imagination.[4] A small comet contains about a *billion tons of ice.* A large comet may contain a *thousand times as much.* At the distant edge of the solar system lies a vast reservoir of comets, called the Oort cloud after its discoverer, the Dutch astronomer Jan Oort. Within the Oort cloud, there are about *1000 billion comets.* In fact, our solar system contains such an immense number of gigantic "dirty snowballs" that if all the comets were to melt, they would supply enough water to fill all the ocean basins on the earth more than *one thousand times.* Terrestrial waters are merely a drop in the bucket when compared with the almost unbelievable quantities of ice contained in the comets.

Extraterrestrial water is not limited to the comets. The recent space probes have revealed quantities of ice almost everywhere in the solar system, from the great polar ice caps of Mars to the rings of Saturn. The interiors of the giant planets Jupiter and Saturn contain an immense quantity of ice (exact proportion still unknown) concentrated in a layer that is nearly *10,000 kilometers thick*.[5] For this reason, the outer planets Jupiter, Saturn, Uranus, and Neptune are often called the "icy planets." Moreover, their large moons are commonly referred to as "icy billiard balls" because the surface of each moon (the Jovian moon Io is an exception) consists of a layer of ice that is generally *hundreds of kilometers thick*.[6] Thus, the outer planets and their moons contain an enormous amount of ice—far more than exists on the earth.

It is now recognized that the vast majority of all the ice and water in the solar system is contained in the comets and in the outer planets and their large moons, with only a tiny fraction being found on the earth in the form of polar ice, the oceans, seas, lakes, and rivers. Nevertheless, this very small quantity of terrestrial water is vital; man could not survive without it.

FORMATION OF THE SOLAR SYSTEM

The branch of astronomy dealing with the origin of the solar system is called cosmogony. There has been much recent progress. *The Cambridge Atlas of Astronomy* reports that "the cosmogony of the Solar System has been rejuvenated since the 1970s thanks to the great space exploration enterprise."[7] The catastrophe theory proposed by Jeans and Jeffreys early in the century has been completely abandoned. It tried to attribute the formation of the planets to a catastrophe which supposedly occurred when a star passed near the sun and pulled out a tidal filament from which the planets were formed.

According to the currently accepted theory of cosmogony, the sun and the planets developed at about the same time from a vast cloud of gas and dust, called the primordial nebula.[8] About five billion years ago, the primordial nebula "collapsed" to form the sun. This was caused by the force of gravity. As the primordial nebula collapsed, it heated up. In fact, the temperature of the newly formed sun was so extremely high that it "ignited" the hydrogen nuclei that are present in abundance in the sun. The "burning" of these hydrogen nuclei is called a thermonuclear reaction.[9] This thermonuclear reaction continues to this very day and is the source of the sun's intense heat and dazzling brightness.

In recent years, astronomers have identified several primordial nebulae in various stages of stellar formation.[10] Therefore, the current theory of the birth of the sun is very firmly established.

The formation of the planets is a much more complex phenomenon.[11] After the sun had formed from the primordial nebula, the remaining material consisted of enormous quantities of gases which surround the sun. These gases, called the solar nebula, would not normally be expected to develop into planets. The *Atlas* explains that "the formation of a planetary system around a star requires special conditions, counteracting the natural tendency to form double or multiple stellar systems."[12] (The nature of these complicated "special conditions" need not concern us here.) Fortunately for man, the solar nebula did satisfy these "special conditions." Therefore, it gradually developed into the planets, their moons, the asteroids, and the comets, which together comprise our planetary system.

The process by which the solar nebula evolved into the planetary system resembles in many ways the familiar phenomenon of the condensation of steam into droplets of water. Before condensation, the gaseous steam entirely fills its container. When condensation occurs, the steam becomes concentrated into small droplets, leaving most of the container completely empty.

By analogy, one can describe the process of planetary formation in similar terms. Before the planets were formed, the gaseous solar nebula filled the entire region around the sun. The planetary system evolved as this solar nebula "condensed" into "clumps" of material—planets, moons, asteroids, and comets. The condensation of the solar nebula thus transformed a giant cloud of gas into the remarkable array of planetary bodies, separated by vast empty spaces, that constitutes our solar system.

THE BIBLICAL TEXT

Having described the process by which the solar system was formed, we are in a position to make a comparison between the biblical text and current scientific knowledge.

The existence of huge quantities of ice in the outer regions of the solar system has become a scientifically established fact. The biblical phrase "the waters which were above the heaven" may be understood to refer to this ice, which is found in the remote comets, in the outer planets, and in their moons. Moreover, this distant ice is separated from terrestrial water ("the waters which were below the heaven") by the vast regions of outer space ("the heaven"). Thus, our solar system can indeed be characterized by "heaven in the midst of the waters."

The preceding discussion indicates that the formation of the solar system is the subject of the second day of creation.[13] The constituents of the planetary system—planets, moons, comets— all evolved from the solar nebula at about the same time. The planetary system was formed by the condensation of the initially gaseous solar nebula into clumps of material, much of it ice and water.

Vast empty spaces opened up in the solar system as the previously homogeneous solar nebula condensed into the planets, moons, and comets. This condensation, or *separation*, of the solar nebula into distinct regions—the *distant* icy planets and comets and the *nearby* terrestrial water—is consistent with the biblical phrase "let it [heaven] separate waters from waters." In the formation of the solar system, "heaven" (outer space) did indeed "separate" the various sources of ice and water.

Enormous advances have taken place in planetary science within the past few decades, producing for the first time a soundly based picture of the origin of the solar system. It is here seen that this recently discovered scientific knowledge provides new understanding for previously enigmatic biblical passages.

AN "ACCIDENTAL OCCURRENCE"

It is worth emphasizing that the formation of the planetary system was by no means a natural development of the solar nebula. Quite the contrary. It is now recognized that the formation of the planets was an unusual event, requiring a special combination of conditions in the solar nebula which are not normally expected to occur.[14] Moreover, even after these special conditions were met and small planetoids did begin to form, it was still unlikely that the embryonic planetoids would continue to grow into planets. However, the relative motions of these small embryos satisfied certain stringent conditions and, as a result, "our Solar System escaped these two misfortunes . . . thus allowing the embryos to grow."[15] The tens of asteroids that orbit around the sun are examples of small embryos that never did "grow" into planets. However, some of the small embryonic planetoids did coalesce to form the full-size planets that exist today, including the planet Earth, which is capable of sustaining life.

Thus, we see that planetary formation, a necessary prerequisite for the existence of man, was the result of a highly unlikely series of events. To a secular scientist, this is merely a fortunate coincidence of nature. However, one who believes in God has a totally different explanation for such very significant "accidental occurrences."

NOTES

1. J. Audouze et al., eds. *The Cambridge Atlas of Astronomy* (Cambridge: At the University Press, 1985), p. 219.

2. Ibid.

3. Ibid., pp. 212–219. This section contains an excellent summary of the properties of comets.

4. Ibid.

5. Ibid., pp. 156–209. This section contains a complete survey of current knowledge of the outer planets. J. K. Beatty et al., eds., *The New Solar System* (Cambridge: At the University Press, 1981). Chapters 12–16 contain a detailed description of the outer planets and their moons.

6. Beatty, et al., chaps. 12–16.

7. Audouze et al., p. 56.

8. Ibid., pp. 56–60. This section describes in detail the scientific evidence in support of the currently accepted theory of the origin of the solar system.

9. Strictly speaking, the hydrogen nuclei (also called protons) in the sun are first transformed into nuclei of heavy hydrogen (also called deuterons). It is the heavy hydrogen nuclei that "burn" in the thermonuclear reaction.

10. Audouze et al., p. 56.

11. Ibid., pp. 56–60.

12. Ibid., p. 58.

13. Since the formation of the solar system is here associated with the second day of creation, the reader may justifiably ask which events are to be associated with the fourth day of creation. This question will be addressed in the chapter dealing with the fourth day of creation.

14. Audouze et al., p. 58.

15. Ibid., p. 59.

The Third Day
The Appearance of Dry
Land and the Plants

GENESIS—CHAPTER I

⁹*And God said, "Let the waters below the heaven be gathered into one place, and let the dry land appear." And it was so.* ¹⁰*And God called the dry land Earth, and the gathering of the waters He called Seas. And God saw that it was good.* ¹¹*And God said, "Let the earth bring forth grass, herb yielding seed, and fruit tree bearing fruit after its kind containing its own seed upon the earth." And it was so.* ¹²*And the earth brought forth grass, herb yielding seed after its kind, and tree bearing fruit containing its own seed after its kind. And God saw that it was good.* ¹³ *And there was evening and there was morning—a third day.*

QUESTIONS

The third day of creation deals with two separate events—the appearance of dry land and the appearance of plant life—which are described in Genesis 1:9–13. The principal geological event depicted in the biblical text seems almost unbelievable.

1. We read that the terrestrial waters suddenly "gathered into one place, and let the dry land appear" (1:9). There is, in fact, not the slightest shred of scientific evidence for any such sudden flowing of the world's oceans and seas. Indeed, the very notion of vast oceanic flows that "let the dry land appear" has more than a touch of fantasy. Moreover, no indication is given in the text of the location of that "one place" to which the oceans presumably flowed.

2. Another puzzling feature of the text concerns the association of a second, completely unrelated subject with the same third day of creation. We read that plant life also appeared on the third day of creation (1:12). Why are these two quite different events—the formation of the dry land and the appearance of plants—linked together? What possible connection could there be between them?

The two points discussed above represent the popular view. We shall now present the recent geological evidence which has greatly enhanced our understanding of the properties of the surface of the earth. These new findings provide an explanation of the biblical text that is consistent with current scientific knowledge.

GEOLOGY

Hardly any feature of our planet seems more stable and secure than the continents. These vast expanses of land—solid bedrock, towering mountains, deep canyons—are the very epitome of permanence and immutability. This is how it seems to the layman, and at one time, so it also seemed to the professional geologist. Therefore, when a little-known German meteorologist named Alfred Wegener proposed in 1912 that entire continents had moved many thousands of kilometers in the distant past, his proposal was greeted with utter disbelief and outright ridicule.[1] Since Wegener was unable to suggest any mechanism that would cause the continents to move, his idea was dismissed by his colleagues. Wegener spent the rest of his life trying, in vain, to win acceptance for his theory of continental drift.

Today, the theory of continental drift is accepted by every geologist, and is generally considered to be one of the most important advances in geology in the twentieth century. This radical change in professional opinion took place as a result of the enormous increase in scientific knowledge amassed by geologists since the early 1960s. This recent knowledge has led to a new, soundly based understanding of many aspects of geology. Professor E. R. Oxburgh of the University of Cambridge has vividly described the current situation in geology in his foreword to the authoritative *Cambridge Encyclopedia of Earth Sciences:*

> It is very seldom that those working in any area of scientific research find themselves caught up in an episode of conceptual change so rapid and so fundamental that external observers of the field begin to use terms such as "scientific revolution" to describe the activity they perceive. Yet this is precisely what has happened in the Earth sciences over the last two decades.[2]

CONTINENTAL DRIFT

The outer layer of the surface of the earth is called the "lithosphere." This layer is about 50 to 100 kilometers thick, a bit thinner under the oceans and a bit thicker under the continents. The well-founded theory of plate tectonics has established that the lithosphere is not a solid shell. Instead, it contains a number of separate plates, many thousands of kilometers in size. Thus, the entire surface of the earth consists of about a dozen large plates which bear all the world's continents and oceans, much as a frog might be borne on a large lily pad. The key point is that the plates themselves do not sit on a solid base, but rather they float on a viscous lower layer, called the "mantle," much as a lily pad floats on pond water. Briefly, the modern geological view is that the continents and oceans (the "frogs") rest on a series of gigantic plates (the "lily pads") which in turn float on the earth's mantle (the "pond").

The most important property of these plates is their ability to move. In fact, if one plate merely rubs against its neighbor, the result can be a devastating earthquake (if under a continent) or a massive tidal wave (if under an ocean). Moreover, the plates can and do move large distances across the surface of the earth in the course of millions of years. This dramatic phenomenon, which results in the large-scale movements of entire continents, is the explanation for Wegener's theory of continental drift.

The map of our planet is familiar; it consists of several large continents separated by wide oceans. But it was not always so. About 250 million years ago, in what geologists call the Permian period (see Appendix A), a single supercontinent named Pangaea stretched across the entire globe from the North Pole to the South Pole. During this period, an entire ocean, named the Iapetus, gradually closed up and disappeared. Such was the map of the earth at the end of the Permian period.

Tens of millions of years later, the supercontinent Pangaea gradually began to break up, and its various sections slowly drifted apart to form the present-day continents and the present-day oceans.

THE PERMIAN PERIOD

Nearly 30 percent of the surface of the earth is dry land, with the remainder being covered with water. But it was not always so. Professor Niles Eldredge, curator at the world-renowned American Museum of Natural History, explains: "These are unusual times. It is far more usual to find the lands flooded, covered with a thin veneer of seawater. . . . Over the last half-billion years, the polar ice caps have generally been smaller, and there has simply been a lot more water to spread out over the earth's surface. . . . Much of the rest of what is now the United States and Canada lay beneath the waves."[3]

The above passage describes the surface of the earth in what geologists call the Devonian period, which preceded by about 100 million years the Permian period described earlier (see Appendix A). Not only did the Devonian seas "spread out over the earth's surface" but the Devonian climate was very warm, so warm in fact that "the seas that covered the land were tropical. Corals, even coral reefs, were abundant, in keeping with the modern observation that massive coral reefs thrive only near the equator. The old epicontinental waterway was warm, shallow and pretty homogeneous over a huge area."[4]

After the Devonian period, the climate cooled dramatically and the Permian period (which began 280 million years ago) experienced one of the most severe ice ages that the world has ever seen.[5] An ice age is characterized by the formation of huge polar ice caps via a process called glaciation. In the Permian ice age, "the center of glaciation was close to the geographical south pole."[6] The polar ice caps "locked up" vast quantities of sea water, causing the sea level to drop significantly. Large new land areas appeared as the seas receded.

The great Permian ice age and the supercontinent Pangaea were not the only special features that marked the Permian period. This period also witnessed the mass extinction of almost all animal life then existent, most of which consisted of marine life that inhabited the warm shallow seas. As the earth cooled during the Permian ice age, and "as the seas gave way to the rising land,"[7] the global catastrophe struck. The Permian period closed "with a mass extinction of perhaps as many as 90% of all living species."[8]

Finally, we come to the last special feature that characterized the Permian period—the proliferation of plant life. The first "plants" had appeared earlier, but these primitive flora were so different from present-day species that they would hardly be recognized as plants by anyone who is not a botanist.[9] Modern-looking green plants first spread over the landscape during the Permian period.

The change in the Permian landscape produced by this green-ery was so striking, *The Cambridge Encyclopedia of Earth Sciences* points out, that "it has been said that the one evolutionary event on Earth that could have been recognized from space was the colonization of the land by plants. The major environmental difference between early and late Paleozoic times must surely be

34

that the land surface during the [earlier] periods was devoid of plant life as we know it."[10] The expression "late Paleozoic times" refers to the Permian period, which is the name geologists have given to the last period of the Paleozoic era (see Appendix A).

THE BIBLICAL TEXT

Having described the series of remarkable and dramatic events that occurred during the time interval known to geologists as the Permian period, we are in a position to make a comparison between the biblical text and current scientific knowledge. We shall relate to the questions that were posed at the beginning of this chapter.

1. In the distant past, the surface of the earth looked entirely different from the way it looks today. Moreover, during the Permian period, an ice age of unprecedented intensity occurred. This ice age caused vast quantities of sea water to freeze and form great polar ice caps. By the end of the Permian period, the oceans had receded, many large seas had disappeared entirely, and *the extent of the dry land greatly increased* ("the seas gave way to the rising land"[11]). These unique events are consistent with the biblical passage "Let the waters below the heaven be gathered into one place, and let the dry land appear" (1:9).

Current knowledge of the Permian ice age enables us to identify the South Pole as the location of the "one place" to which the waters gathered. The disappearance of many seas was caused by the glaciation which resulted in the formation of immense ice caps. It has now been established that during the Permian ice age, "the center of glaciation was close to the geographic south pole."[12]

2. The Permian period was also characterized by the proliferation of plant life on earth. The Permian "colonization of the land by plants" was so striking that it has been termed by the *Cambridge Encyclopedia of Earth Sciences* as the "major environmental difference" between the Permian period and earlier periods which were "devoid of plant life as we know it."[13]

These two events—the marked increase in the dry land area ("let the dry land appear") and the first appearance of a green floral landscape ("let the earth bring forth grass")—*both* occurred during the same geological time period. Therefore, it is appropriate that the biblical text should associate both with the same third day of creation.

AN "ACCIDENTAL OCCURRENCE"

No discussion of the oceans and seas should conclude without mentioning that the very existence of oceans and seas on the planet Earth is a remarkable "accidental occurrence." This can best be appreciated by comparing our own planet Earth with our neighboring planets Mars and Venus.

Shortly after they were formed about 4.6 billion years ago, all three planets (Earth, Mars, and Venus) had comparable amounts of surface water. In fact, the deep channels that are observed today on the surface of Mars were carved out long ago by the copious, fast-flowing Martian primordial surface waters.[14] Moreover, it has recently been established that "originally, the atmosphere of Mars must have been relatively hot and it would certainly have contained large quantities of water."[15] Note that this description of Mars in its early history is quite similar to our own planet. Why, then, are the two planets so completely different today?

The difference in the subsequent development of Mars and Earth was due to the fact that Mars is somewhat more distant from the Sun than the Earth. This caused the temperature of Mars to drop in the course of time. Eventually, Mars became so cold that all its surface water froze, most of it forming gigantic polar ice caps. Since the Martian temperature will forever remain below the freezing point of water, these polar ice caps will never thaw, and they have become a striking permanent feature of the Martian landscape. As a result, the planet Mars has become completely devoid of all liquid water, thus preventing the existence of life as we know it on that planet.

Our other neighbor, Venus, is somewhat closer to the Sun than the Earth and therefore has had a completely different history. Originally, Venus was very similar to the Earth in that Venus was once covered by deep oceans which contained the equivalent of a layer of water 3 kilometers deep over the entire surface of the planet.[16] But its proximity to the Sun caused

Venus gradually to become hotter. This led to a peculiar atmospheric phenomenon known as the "runaway greenhouse effect," which causes the retention of almost all the energy impinging on the planet from the Sun.[17] As a result, the surface temperature of Venus rose to its present enormous value of 460°C. When Venus became so intensely hot, all its oceans and seas completely evaporated and then decomposed into hydrogen gas and oxygen gas, both of which later dissipated. Therefore, "there is now practically no water on Venus. . . . only its greater proximity to the Sun, by setting off the runaway greenhouse effect, prevented Venus from later developing an atmosphere like the Earth's."[18]

In summary, Earth, Mars, and Venus were all once covered with vast oceans and each had an atmosphere conducive to life. However, the development of Mars and Venus were such that on both these planets, all surface water disappeared in the course of time and their atmospheres became completely hostile to life. Why did the Earth escape these catastrophes? And they are properly termed catastrophes, because man cannot survive without water.

The answer is that the Earth escaped these catastrophes by sheer accident! The Earth *just happened* to be sufficiently distant from the Sun that the runaway greenhouse effect did not occur and therefore all our surface water neither evaporated nor decomposed. Moreover, the Earth *just happened* to be sufficiently near the Sun that it remained warm enough to prevent all the oceans from freezing permanently into ice caps. Therefore, the Earth *alone*, among the planets of the solar system, is capable of supporting human life. It is quite remarkable that the Earth is precisely the required distance from the Sun to support human life, being neither too far (as is Mars) nor too near (as is Venus). This enigmatic situation has come to be known among scientists as the "Goldilocks problem of climatology."[19]

Recent studies of the carbonate-silicate geochemical cycle have made it increasingly clear that the planetary atmosphere is controlled by a very delicate balance, involving the subtle interplay of many factors, which determines whether or not life can exist.[20] This balance is so delicate that if the Earth were only a few percent closer to the Sun, surface temperatures would be far higher than the boiling point of water, precluding all possibility of life.[21] Similarly, if the Earth were only a few percent farther from the Sun, the concentration of carbon dioxide in the atmosphere would be so high that "the atmosphere would not be breathable by human beings."[22] Thus, the orbit of the Earth *just happened* to be at a distance from the Sun that is in "a very narrow habitable zone within which liquid water could condense. . . . life could appear in this extremely narrow zone."[23]

In the chapter dealing with the second day of creation, we focused attention on the series of "accidental occurrences" that were necessary for the formation of the planets. Here, we see that yet another series of "accidental occurrences" is necessary for the existence of the oceans and seas, lying beneath a breathable atmosphere. Indeed, it has become increasingly obvious in recent years that there are a great many quite stringent requirements of nature that are necessary—and somehow *just happen* to occur—for the survival of man. This phenomenon has attracted considerable scientific interest and has been named the "anthropic principle."[24] However, the believing person would probably find this phenomenon more accurately described as the "divine principle," in accordance with the biblical expression "It is the finger of God" (Exodus 8:15).

NOTES

1. A. Hallam, *Scientific American*, vol. 232, February 1975, pp. 88–97. An amusing account of the history of Wegener's theory of continental drift has been given by J. M. Ziman, *The Force of Knowledge* (Cambridge: At the University Press, 1976), pp. 79–81.

2. D. G. Smith, chief ed., *The Cambridge Encyclopedia of Earth Sciences* (Cambridge: At the University Press, 1981), p. 6. This standard reference work on earth sciences contains a comprehensive account of all aspects of geology.

3. N. Eldredge, *Time Frames* (New York: Simon & Schuster, 1985), p. 38.

4. Ibid., p. 39.

5. Smith, p. 299.

6. Ibid.

7. Eldredge, p. 40.

8. Ibid., p. 39.

9. Smith, p. 377.

10. Ibid., p. 405.

11. Eldredge, p. 40.

12. Smith, p. 299.

13. Ibid., p. 405.

14. J. Audouze et al., eds., *The Cambridge Atlas of Astronomy* (Cambridge: At the University Press, 1985), pp. 124–149. This section contains a complete survey of current knowledge of Martian topography.

15. Ibid., p. 126.

16. Ibid., pp. 70–81. This section contains an excellent summary of the surface features of Venus.

17. Ibid., p. 73.

18. Ibid., p. 63.

19. J. F. Kasting et al., *Scientific American*, vol. 258, February 1988, p. 46.

20. Ibid., pp. 46–53.

21. Audouze et al., p. 63.

22. Kasting et al., p. 53.

23. Audouze et al., p. 63.

24. J. D. Barrow and F. J. Tipler, *The Anthropic Cosmological Principle* (Oxford: At the University Press, 1986). G. Gale, *Scientific American*, vol. 245, December 1981, pp. 114–122.

The Fourth Day
The Seasons, the Days, and the Years

GENESIS—CHAPTER I

¹⁴*And God said, "Let there be luminaries in the firmament of the heaven to separate the day from the night; and let them be for signs, for the seasons, for the days and the years;* ¹⁵*and let them be for luminaries in the firmament of the heaven to give light upon the earth." And it was so.* ¹⁶*And God made the two large luminaries—the large luminary to rule the day and the small luminary to rule the night—and the stars.* ¹⁷*And God set them in the firmament of the heaven to give light upon the earth,* ¹⁸*and to rule during the day and during the night, and to separate the light from the darkness. And God saw that it was good.* ¹⁹*And there was evening and there was morning—a fourth day.*

QUESTIONS

The fourth day of creation deals with the sun and the moon and their functions in the heaven, as described in Genesis 1:14–19. The biblical text raises the following questions.

1. In an earlier chapter, we proposed that the formation of the solar system, including the sun and the moon, was associated with the second day of creation. If so, what astronomical event is to be associated with the fourth day of creation?

2. We read that the functions of the sun and the moon include determining "the seasons, the days and the years." (1:14). It is clear that the sun performs these functions, but why is the moon also mentioned? The moon has no effect whatever on the length of the day or the year; these are both determined solely by the motion of the earth relative to the sun. Moreover, the notion that the moon in some way influences the seasons and the weather has its origin in old superstitions, long discarded by educated people.

3. The sun and the moon are first referred to as "the two large luminaries" (1:16), but immediately afterwards in the same verse, they are referred to as "the large luminary" (sun) and "the small luminary" (moon). Why are the sun and the moon first *incorrectly* described as if they were of comparable size, and only afterwards correctly described as the "large" sun and the "small" moon? Any handbook of the solar system will confirm that the sun is 400 times larger than the moon.

We shall now present the scientific evidence which provides an explanation of the biblical text that is consistent with current scientific knowledge.

THE DAY, THE YEAR, AND THE SEASONS

Few statements seem more firmly established than the assertions that the day has twenty-four hours, that the year has 365 days, that a compass needle always points north, and that in the Northern Hemisphere, the summer begins in June and the winter in December. But it was not always so. Geological evidence has established that in the middle of the Paleozoic era, the day had only 21 hours and the year had more than 400 days.[1] Moreover, recent studies of magnetic sediments on the ocean floor have shown that a million years ago, compass needles pointed south.[2] Finally, the Northern Hemisphere summer once started in December and the winter in June.[3]

If the solar system consisted only of the sun and a spherical earth, then neither the length of the day nor the number of days in a year would ever change, and June would always herald the onset of summer.[4] In fact, however, the earth is also subject to the gravitational attraction of the moon. (The gravitational attraction of the distant planets is slight.) As a result, the motion of the earth is not limited to its primary motions of rotating about its axis and revolving around the sun. Because of the moon's gravitational attraction, the earth also undergoes important secondary motions. It is precisely these complex secondary motions of the earth that are responsible for the changes in the day, the year, and the seasons.[5]

The gradual changes in the motion of the earth that are caused by the moon may seem to the layman to be mere esoteric details, no doubt very interesting to the professional astronomer, but of no great practical consequence. We shall show how incorrect such an assessment is. Indeed, it is not too much to say that the very fabric of human existence has been decisively altered by the seemingly minor changes that the moon has caused in the motion of the earth.

THE ICE AGE AND THE HOLOCENE EPOCH

The earth is a warm, pleasant, hospitable planet, whose mild climate is conducive to man's physical well-being and cultural development. But it was not always so. Only 18,000 years ago, our planet was caught in the grip of a savage ice age. Fully one third of the land area lay buried beneath massive glaciers whose thickness was measured in kilometers.[6] The glaciers extended so far south that the ground beneath the present-day metropolitan centers of New York, London, Paris, and Berlin was covered by thick sheets of ice.

About 10,000 years ago, the severity of the ice age began to subside.[7] The glaciers retreated, temperatures began to rise, and the ice sheets melted. In the course of this deglaciation, a milder climate gradually spread over most of the globe. Meteorological evidence shows that as the land was freed from the ice, profound worldwide changes occurred in the weather. There was a "renewed rise in temperature setting in at 10,000 BP [BP = years before present] which led to the sustained warm climate of postglacial times . . . during the period 9000–8000 BP, temperatures continued to rise . . . the colder seasons of the year gradually became milder . . . summers became gradually warmer."[8] The fierce ice age was over; the earth had entered the warm interglacial period that continues to the present day.

The changes in human society that occurred after the debilitating ice age ended were so striking that scientists have designated the current interglacial period by a special name—the Holocene epoch. The emphasis of this name is *not* on the marked changes in climate, but rather on the extensive evidence of man's accelerated cultural development. *The Cambridge Encyclopedia of Archaeology* explains: "The latest warm interval, which began 10,000 years ago and is still continuing, is conventionally referred as the Holocene. . . . This distinction, emphasizing the uniqueness of the last 10,000 years, is more important in terms of cultural development than of climatic pattern."[9]

THE MILANKOVITCH THEORY OF ICE AGES

The glaciation of 18,000 years ago and the subsequent deglaciation of 10,000 years ago were the most recent of the ten ice ages that have occurred during the past million years. What causes this recurrent cycle of an ice age followed by a warm interglacial period? Of the various theories proposed, it has recently become clear that "a growing body of evidence strongly supports one idea: ice ages are caused by small changes in the tilt of the earth's axis and in the geometry of the earth's orbit around the sun."[10] This conclusion is based on "studies of sedimentary deposits in the earth's oceans" which have shown that "these astronomical variations . . . played a key role in causing these recent dramatic changes in climate."[11]

The Yugoslavian astronomer Milutin Milankovitch was the first to propose that small periodic changes in the motion of the earth are the cause of the recurrent cycle of an ice age followed by a warm interglacial period. The Milankovitch theory relates the world's climate to three parameters that characterize the earth's orbit: (1) the degree to which the elliptical orbit departs from a perfect circle, called the "eccentricity"; (2) the angle between the earth's axis of rotation and the direction perpendicular to the plane of its orbit, called the "axial obliquity" or the "tilt"; and (3) the direction in which the axis points when the earth is closest to the sun, called the "season of perihelion."[12]

Although the Milankovitch theory was proposed more than half a century ago, "only within the past 10 years has enough evidence accumulated to convince the majority of earth scientists that there is a connection between the ice ages and the [earth's] orbit."[13] The "decisive evidence" in favor of the Milankovitch theory was established in 1976 by Hays, Imbrie, and Shackleton.[14] For his important contribution in proving the Milankovitch theory of ice ages, Professor John Imbrie received in 1986 the prestigious Ewing Award of the American Geophysical Union.

We close this discussion by emphasizing that each of the three orbit parameters that is central to the Milankovitch theory "changes with time as a result of the small gravitational pull of the moon."[15] In this way, the moon exerts a decisive influence on the weather and on the seasons that we experience here on earth.

APPARENT SIZE OF ASTRONOMICAL BODIES

An astronomical body is characterized both by its true size and its apparent size. The apparent size of an astronomical body specifies how large it *appears* to an observer on the earth. Therefore, the apparent size of an object is given by the ratio of its true size to its distance from the earth. It is measured by the angle that the object subtends at the position of a terrestrial observer.

Applying this concept to the sun and the moon, one finds a

most remarkable coincidence. The apparent sizes of the sun and the moon are *exactly* the same. Each of these astronomical bodies has an apparent size of 0.53°. Although the diameter of the sun is 400 times larger than that of the moon, the sun is also 400 times farther away from the earth. This equality in apparent size is most striking during a total eclipse of the sun. The fact that the disk of the moon *exactly* covers the disk of the sun—being neither larger nor smaller—is responsible for the dramatic visual effect that so enthralls every observer of a total solar eclipse.

THE BIBLICAL TEXT

Having discussed the Milankovitch theory of ice ages and the astronomical concept of apparent size, we are in a position to make a comparison between the biblical text and current scientific knowledge with regard to each of the questions that were raised at the beginning of this chapter.

1. When the solar system was first formed (the event associated with the second day of creation), the number of hours in a day was far fewer than 24 and the number of days in a year was far greater than 365. Moreover, the seasons had little resemblence to the present-day succession of spring, summer, autumn, and winter. It was only relatively recently that the orbit of the Earth reached its present configuration. This configuration is responsible for our day of 24 hours, our year of 365 days, and the mild seasons found in most areas of our planet.

The fixing of the seasons, the days, and the years by the present-day relative positions of the sun, the moon, and the earth is the event associated with the fourth day of creation. This is the meaning of the biblical passage "Let there be luminaries in the heaven . . . for the seasons, for the days and the years" (1:14).

2. The moon has played a central role in fixing the length of the day and the number of days in the year. Moreover, according to the well-established Milankovitch theory, the moon's gravitational attraction is responsible for the present-day mild climate that has been so conducive to man's unprecedented cultural, intellectual, and technological development. Therefore, the biblical text that lists the moon among the astronomical bodies that

determine "the seasons, the days and the years" is consistent with current scientific knowledge.

3. Like all astronomical bodies, the sun and the moon are described both by their true size and by their apparent size. It is an astronomical fact that the apparent sizes of the sun and the moon are *exactly* the same. Thus, the biblical passage that describes the sun and moon as "the two large luminaries" (1:16), as if they were the same size, may be understood as referring to their apparent sizes, which are in fact exactly equal. The subsequent biblical passage that describes the sun as "the large luminary" and the moon as "the small luminary" refers to their true sizes.

"ACCIDENTAL OCCURRENCES"

No discussion of the moon should conclude without mentioning that its very existence is the result of a series of "accidental occurrences." It was recently shown by Professor A. G. W. Cameron of Harvard University that the moon resulted from "the impact on the Earth of a planetary body a little larger than Mars."[16] Computer simulations have established how our moon was formed from remnants of the collison between a planetary body and the earth. Our moon is thus *unique*, having been formed by a process quite different from that responsible for the formation of the other moons of the solar system.

It should be emphasized that the detailed computer calculations of Professor Cameron and his colleagues have demonstrated that the moon would *not* have resulted from a collison between planetary bodies unless certain stringent conditions were met. Our moon was formed from a planetary collision because the colliding body *just happened* to have the required mass, *just happened* to have the required relative velocity and angle of collision, and *just happened* to have the required composition for its core and mantle. If these constraints on the motion and composition of the colliding body had not been satisfied, then the collision would have been shattering and no moon would have formed.

We reiterate that the moon is not merely an attractive orna-
ment that decorates the night sky. The moon has played a crucial
role in producing and maintaining the present mild climate on
the earth. The weather we now enjoy is completely different
from the extremely harsh climate that prevailed during the
preceding ice age. The mild climate of the past few thousand
years has permitted the flourishing of human society. Indeed,
the condition of man's existence has been decisively altered by
the many profound cultural changes that have occurred since the
end of the ice age. Impressive accomplishments have been recorded in every sphere of human endeavor. Major technological
advances have transformed man from a modest inhabitant of the
earth to the triumphant conqueror of the moon—all within the
short span of a few thousand years. This unprecedented blos-
soming of human activity, leading to man's accelerated cultural
development, has been made possible by the recent dramatic
improvement in the weather worldwide. And the weather we
experience today is directly related to the influence of the moon
on the earth.

NOTES

1. J. Audouze et al., eds., *The Cambridge Atlas of Astronomy* (Cambridge: At the University Press, 1985), p. 54.

2. D. G. Smith, chief ed., *The Cambridge Encyclopedia of Earth Sciences* (Cambridge: At the University Press, 1981), p. 120.

3. J. G. Lookwood, *World Climate Systems* (London: Edward Arnold, 1985), p. 110.

4. H. Goldstein, *Classical Mechanics*, 2 ed. (Reading, Mass.: Addison-Wesley, 1980), secs. 3.7–3.8.

5. Smith, p. 120. C. Covey, *Scientific American*, vol. 250, February 1984, pp. 42–50.

6. C. Covey, pp. 42–50.

7. H. H. Lamb, *Climate: Present, Past and Future* (London: Methuen, 1977), vol. 2, chap. 16.

8. Ibid., pp. 371–372.

9. A. Sherrant, ed., *The Cambridge Encyclopedia of Archaeology* (Cambridge: At the University Press, 1980), p. 52.

10. Covey, p. 42.

11. J. K. Beatty et al., eds., *The New Solar System* (Cambridge: At the University Press, 1981), p. 69.

12. Lookwood, p. 110. Covey, pp. 42–50.

13. Covey, p. 47.

14. J. D. Hays, J. Imbrie, and N. J. Shackleton, *Science*, vol. 194, December 1976, pp. 1121–1132.

15. Covey, p. 45.

16. "Science and the Citizen," *Scientific American*, vol. 254, June 1986, pp. 67–68.

The Fifth Day (Part I)
Evolution

GENESIS—CHAPTER I

²⁰*And God said, "Let the waters swarm with living creatures, and let winged creatures fly above the earth across the firmament of the heaven." ²¹And God created the large sea-creatures and every living creature that crawls, with which the waters swarmed, after its kind, and every winged creature after its kind. And God saw that it was good. ²²And God blessed them, saying, "Be fruitful and multiply, and fill the waters in the seas, and let the winged creatures proliferate on land." ²³And there was evening and there was morning—a fifth day.*

²⁴*And God said, "Let the earth bring forth the living creature after its kind: cattle, and the crawling creature, and the beast of the land after its kind." And it was so. ²⁵ And God made the beast of the land after its kind, and the cattle after its kind, and every living thing that crawls on the ground after its kind. And God saw that it was good.*

QUESTIONS

The event associated with the fifth day and the beginning of the sixth day of creation is the formation of the animal kingdom. There are three topics that require discussion (1) Darwin's theory of evolution, (2) the origin of life, and (3) the specific description given in the biblical text for the formation of the animals. Each of these topics merits a separate chapter. Here we take up the question of evolution.

The question that is most commonly asked about Genesis 1:20–25 is that these six verses appear to contradict Darwin's theory of evolution, probably the most widely known theory in all of science. The question is usually phrased in the following way:

Darwin's theory of evolution explains how primitive species gradually evolved during the eons of geologic time into the vast panorama of animals that we observe today. Darwin's theory not only appears convincing, it has also been buttressed by an extensive array of fossil evidence amassed in the course of detailed studies by many scientists. As a result, Darwin's theory of evolution is today accepted throughout the scientific world. The only doubters are a small group known as "creationists," who object on religious grounds. But on scientific grounds, Darwin's theory is not disputed.

In contrast to Darwin's theory of evolution, the biblical account asserts a separate divine act of creation for every species of animal known today. Indeed, the very notion that animals have evolved gradually, with all present-day animals originating from preexisting forms, is inconsistent with the text of Genesis.

The foregoing paragraphs represent the popular view. In this chapter, we shall demonstrate that this view is flawed in two respects. First, the extensive fossil evidence now available shows that, far from being conclusively proved, Darwin's theory of evolution is incompatible with current scientific data. Secondly, careful reading shows that the biblical text is, in fact, consistent with the idea that present-day animals developed from earlier animals. We shall now discuss each of these two points.

DARWIN'S THEORY OF EVOLUTION

When discussing the scientific evidence relating to Darwin's theory of evolution, one must carefully distinguish between the *fact* that many species have become extinct and many new species have appeared and the *theory* proposed to explain this change in species.[1] The *fact* that species change was known from the fossil record long before Darwin's famous book *On the Origin of Species* appeared in 1859. Darwin's book introduced the *theory* that species gradually evolve from one to another through such agencies as the survival of the fittest, the struggle for existence, natural selection, and adaptation. It should be noted that in current usage, the term "Darwin's theory of evolution" encompasses the incorporation of modern genetic theory and population biology into Darwin's original theory. And this will be the meaning of the term throughout this volume. This synthesis is often called the synthetic theory of evolution or neo-Darwinism.[2]

A key point of Darwin's explanation is that evolution works in small cumulative steps through vast periods of time to make primitive species gradually evolve into more complex species. However, if this explanation is correct, then the transitional forms between one type of animal and another must also appear in the fossil record. The fact is that these predicted transitional forms have never been found.[3]

Darwin was well aware of this problem, to which he devoted an entire chapter of his book (chap. X), writing, "Why then is not every geological formation and every stratum full of such intermediate links? . . . This, perhaps, is the most obvious and serious objection which can be urged against the theory."[4] His answer was that "the explanation lies, as I believe, in the extreme imperfection of the geological record."[5]

Darwin's answer may have been plausible in 1859, but surely not in 1989. The geological record of fossils has been vastly improved during the last century, and it has become abundantly clear that the predicted fossils of the transitional forms do not exist. Professor Stephen J. Gould of Harvard University reveals that "The extreme rarity of transitional forms in the fossil record persists as the trade secret of paleontology."[6] Gould emphasizes that "The evolutionary trees that adorn our textbooks are not the evidence of fossils and . . . are never 'seen' in the rocks."[7] Similarly, Professor Niles Eldredge, Curator at the American Museum of Natural History, points out that the fossil data clearly show that "large groups—say the orders of mammals (for example, rodents, elephants, carnivores)—appeared too suddenly in the fossil record to admit a rational explanation in terms of gradual adaptive modification."[8] In the same vein, Professor Steven M. Stanley of Johns Hopkins University describes "the general failure of the fossil record to display gradual transitions from one major group to another."[9]

The decisive importance of the lack of transitional forms for Darwin's theory was unequivocally stated by Darwin himself: "He who rejects this view of the imperfection of the geological record, will rightly reject the whole theory."[10]

A second serious difficulty with Darwin's proposal that species evolve gradually is that the "small cumulative steps" that are the backbone of Darwin's theory never occur. The fossil record shows that species appear *suddenly*, disappear just as *suddenly*, and hardly evolve at all. The scientific evidence has been clearly summed up by Professor Steven M. Stanley, one of the world's leading paleontologists, in his recent book *The New Evolutionary Timetable*: "The fossil record reveals that species typically survive for a hundred thousand generations, or even a million or more, without evolving very much"; and further on the same page, "After their origin, most species undergo little evolution before becoming extinct."[11] Professor Gould emphasizes the importance of this recent evidence: "The history of most fossil species includes two features particularly inconsistent with gradualism: (1) *Statis*—species appear in the fossil record looking much the same as when they disappear. (2) *Sudden appearance*—a species does not arise gradually; it appears [in the fossil record] all at once and fully formed."[12]

The sudden, nonevolutionary, indeed catastrophic disappearance of nearly a million species at the same time has become an accepted fact to every professional biologist. The respected *Scientific American* has summarized the evidence in two recent articles, entitled "Mass Extinctions in the Late Mesozoic"[13] and

"Mass Extinctions in the Ocean."[14] Recent research has revealed that no fewer than *seven* such mass extinctions have occurred.[15] In fact, all the world's dinosaurs, together with most other then-existing species, disappeared so suddenly that Nobel laureate Professor Luis W. Alvarez and his colleagues at the University of California have suggested that a giant meteor from outer space collided with the earth to cause this worldwide catastrophe.[16] This proposed explanation for the mass extinctions—the impact of meteors or comets colliding with the earth—is known as the "impact theory."

The scientific evidence in support of the impact theory of Alvarez and co-workers has been summarized in *Physics Today*, the bulletin of the American Physical Society. The bulletin article, entitled "Astronomical Causes of Biological Extinctions", concludes with the statement that "the idea of astronomically caused catastrophes is a tremendously important one to evolutionary biologists."[17] Professor David M. Raup of the University of Chicago has explained the important implications of the impact theory for evolutionary biology in an article, which is appropriately entitled: "Extinctions: Bad Genes or Bad Luck?"[18] In his analysis of such catastrophes, Professor Raup points out that if "the extinction of a given species or higher group is more bad luck than bad genes . . . . [then] the conventional Darwinian model is not correct."[19] and again "pure chance would favor some biologic groups over others—all in the absence of conventional Darwinian selection between species."[20] The important role played by luck in mass extinctions has also been emphasized by Professor S. J. Gould of Harvard University: "If extinctions can demolish more than 90% of all species, then we must be losing groups forever by pure bad luck."[21]

The point is simply put: In mass extinctions, large groups of animals become extinct primarily because of bad luck rather than bad genes. Therefore, the Darwinian concept of natural selection is irrelevant to such extinctions.

It is worth elaborating on this important point. A central feature of Darwin's theory is that certain individuals die while others survive because the surviving individuals are on the average more successful in coping with the local environment (survival of the fittest) than those who perish (natural selection). Moreover, Darwin emphasized that the mechanism that he proposed to explain evolution is a *gradual* one, working in "small cumulative steps" over very long periods of time, typically *millions of years*. The opposite point of view is embodied in the above-mentioned impact theory of Professor Alvarez. According to this theory, the mechanism for the mass extinction of species is due to extraterrestial causes (the impact of meteors or comets colliding with the earth). Thus, the destructive process is *unconnected* with the local environment (*no* natural selection, *no* survival of the fittest). Moreover, the time period for the occurrence of a mass extinction is exceedingly *short*. Alvarez refers to "a span of 1 to 10 years, as predicted by the impact hypothesis."[22]

It therefore follows that the idea that most extinct species were killed off by the impact of meteors is inconsistent with Darwin's theory of evolution.

Darwin himself would have undoubtedly agreed with the above assessment. He emphasized that according to his theory, "The extinction of old forms is the almost inevitable consequence of the production of new forms."[23] And if this proves not to be the case, as the well-documented mass extinctions have now established, Darwin concludes that it would be "a fatal objection to the belief in the transmutation of species. . . . the fact would be fatal to the theory of evolution through natural selection."[24]

The evidence in favor of the Alvarez impact theory is accumulating rapidly. There are now *fifteen* different pieces of scientific data that support this theory.[25] The most convincing evidence is provided by the anomalously large concentrations of iridium (100 times more than expected) found worldwide in sediments that date from the geologic time known as the Cretaceous-Tertiary boundary (see Appendix A). The wealth of recent data which confirm the impact theory led Professor Alvarez to the following definitive statement: "I see no way to escape the conclusion that the Cretaceous-Tertiary extinctions, including that of the dinosaurs, were triggered by the impact of a 10-km-diameter bolide [meteor] . . . This is the only existing theory that agrees with all the observations."[26]

Professor Stephen J. Gould and Professor Niles Eldredge are so convinced by the fossil evidence against gradualism that they have introduced the concept of "punctuated equilibria" to describe the fossil record.[27] This record now reveals the sudden appearance of new species, their existence for very long periods of time without undergoing significant evolutionary changes, and their sudden disappearance.[28] All these facts taken together constitute "the model of 'punctuated equilibria,' which has recently become widely accepted," according to the authoritative *Cambridge Encyclopedia of Earth Sciences.*[29]

The proposal of Darwin that species evolved gradually is currently being attacked on all fronts. Professor S. M. Stanley of Johns Hopkins University has emphasized the striking differences between the current fossil data and the theory of the gradual evolution of species, writing, "Darwin and the many architects of the Modern Synthesis [neo-Darwinism] would have been confounded by the fossil evidence."[30] Professor Niles Eldredge dismisses the idea that the vast panorama of present-day life forms evolved gradually, because "gradual evolution just does not get anywhere in producing the truly new."[31] Professor Kenneth Hsu of the Swiss Institute of Technology points out that further evidence that ' many lifeforms became extinct suddenly and simultaneously worldwide" comes from the stratigraphic studies of magnetic sediments on the ocean floor. He concludes that "magnetostratigraphic investigations in the last few years have certainly dealt the final blow to Darwin's postulate."[32] Even more forceful are the words of Professor Ernst Chain, Nobel laureate from the University of Oxford, who asserts quite unambiguously that "survival of the fittest seems to me a hypothesis based on no evidence and irreconcilable with the facts."[33] Finally, we quote Professor S. J. Gould of Harvard University, whose words go right to the heart of the matter. After ridiculing the widespread tendency to attribute "near omnipotence to natural selection," Professor Gould notes sarcastically that "Darwin has attained sainthood (if not divinity) among evolutionary biologists."[34]

In view of all the recent scientific evidence, it is difficult to understand the biologists' determined defense of Darwin's theory of evolution, often by attributing to Charles Darwin modern ideas that are the direct opposite of what he wrote. Ironically, among the ardent Darwinists, one finds the very scientists who have contributed the most to establishing the evidence that undermines the theory of the gradual evolution of species.

In conclusion, it should be emphasized that no one is attacking Charles Darwin. One need only read *On the Origin of Species* to realize what a great scientist Charles Darwin was. He produced a new comprehensive theory that admirably accounted for the evidence known *at that time*—in the best scientific tradition. But 130 years have passed, our store of scientific knowledge has vastly increased, and Darwin's theory of evolution will simply no longer do. Men like Alvarez, Gould, Stanley, Eldredge, Raup, and Hsu are serious scientists of the first rank. When they tell us that the current scientific data are completely different from the "old facts," we would do well to lay aside our biases and listen. It is time to move forward.

"EVOLUTION OF MAN"

We conclude our discussion with some comments about the "evolution of man." Here, too, the scientific evidence is against the Darwinian concept of gradual evolution. Modern Man (*Homo sapiens sapiens*) appeared suddenly and has "persisted to the present with no apparent change."[35] Thus, Modern Man has undergone no evolutionary change. The species most closely related to Modern Man is Neanderthal Man, who disappeared suddenly shortly before the appearance of Modern Man (see Appendix B). Are there any signs of evolutionary change in Neanderthal Man? Professor Stanley points out that "*Homo neanderthalensis* existed for perhaps 65,000 years with no visible change."[36] Finally, is there any connection between Modern Man and Neanderthal Man? Stanley emphasizes that Modern Man appeared "out of nowhere . . . with particular features that are utterly unpredictable on the basis of what preceded them."[37] This recent evidence is also discussed in a *Scientific American* article entitled "The Neanderthals."[38]

Our discussion of the hominids—the "man-like" species—has been restricted to those species for which the fossil record is very well documented. Current understanding of the earlier hominids is in a state of disarray. New fossil evidence has made it completely unclear just which hominid species preceded which.[39] This point is emphasized in a recent article in the respected British journal *Nature*, carrying the somewhat satirical title, "Who Is the 'Real' *Homo habilis*?"[40] The article characterizes the current state of confusion in the following words: "The new find rudely exposes how little we know about the early evolution of *Homo*."

THE BIBLICAL TEXT

Two different verbs occur in the biblical account of the origin of the animal kingdom. Regarding the formation of the primeval sea creatures, we read in Genesis that God *created* them (1:21), whereas regarding the subsequently formed land animals, we read that God *made* them (1:25). The verbs "create" and "make" clearly denote two quite different processes. Creation implies the formation of something *fundamentally new*, either physically (as in creation *ex nihilo*) or conceptually (as in the creation of a new kind of entity, such as life). By contrast, the process of making implies the fashioning of something *complex* from something *simple* (as in the making of furniture from pieces of wood).

The above discussion suggests the following interpretation of the biblical text. The first expression, "God created," relating to the sea creatures, may be understood as referring to the creation of animal life itself, which initially appeared as marine species with which "the waters swarmed." The subsequent expression, "God made," relating to the land animals, may be understood as referring to the formation of different terrestrial species from the early marine species.

This interpretation of the biblical text, which does not deviate from the literal meaning, incorporates the notion that present-day animals developed from earlier species. This is, in fact, the view proposed by several traditional biblical commentators. Particular mention should be made of Malbim's detailed analysis of verses 1:20–25. Malbim emphasizes that there is no inconsistency at all between the modern concept that animal species have changed in the course of time and the biblical account of the formation of the animals.

NOTES

1. Important new evidence for the fact that species have changed is derived from molecular biology. Studies of mutation rates in the genetic material (DNA) have established relationships between different species. This is called the "protein clock" or the "molecular clock" for DNA. A discussion of these results and their interpretation can be found in a recent *Scientific American* article (October 1985, pp. 148–157).

2. The synthetic theory of evolution provides the answer to three basic questions to which Darwin had no explanation: (1) What is the mechanism that gives rise to the all-important variations in the population that are central to the theory of evolution? (2) Why do these variations not "blend out" in subsequent generations and therefore become diluted to oblivion? (3) How do these variations propagate through the population? None of these three questions relates to the discussion in this chapter, nor do any other aspects of the synthetic theory that are not already present in Darwin's original theory. Therefore, every objection raised here applies with equal force to Darwin's original theory of evolution and to the modern synthetic theory.

3. The famous long-standing problem of the absence of transitional forms relates to the major taxonomic groups, at the level of the phylum, class, and order. At the much lower taxonomic level of the genus and species, there are many examples of transitional forms. However, the major challenge to the theory of evolution is to explain the large-scale changes that lead from one order or class to another.

4. C. Darwin, *On the Origin of Species* (1859; reprint ed., New York: Mentor, 1963), p. 287.

5. Ibid., p. 288.

6. S. J. Gould, *The Panda's Thumb* (New York: Viking Penguin, 1980), p. 150.

7. Ibid., p. 151.

8. N. Eldredge, *Time Frames* (New York: Simon & Schuster, 1985), p. 146.

9. S. M. Stanley, *The New Evolutionary Timetable* (New York: Basic Books, 1981), p. 77.

10. Darwin, p. 336.

11. Stanley, p. xv.

12. Gould, p. 151.

13. D. A. Russell, *Scientific American*, vol. 246, January 1982, pp. 48–55.

14. S. M. Stanley, *Scientific American*, vol. 250, June 1984, pp. 46–54.

15. Ibid., p. 48.

16. W. Alvarez et al., *Science*, vol. 223, March 1984, pp. 1135–1140.

17. H. L. Shipman, *Physics Today*, vol. 38, January 1985, pp. S10–11.

18. D. M. Raup, *Acta Geologica Hispanica*, vol. 15, 1981, pp. 25–33.

19. Ibid., p. 26.

20. Ibid., p. 29.

21. S. J. Gould, *The Flamingo's Smile* (New York: Viking Penguin, 1985), p. 242.

22. Alvarez, p. 1136.

23. Darwin, p. 336.

24. Ibid., p. 305.

25. L. W. Alvarez, *Physics Today*, vol. 40, July 1987, pp. 24–33.

26. Ibid., pp. 30, 33.

27. Eldredge, chap. 4.

28. Stanley, *New Evolutionary Timetable*, chaps. 5–6.

29. D. G. Smith, chief ed., *The Cambridge Encyclopedia of Earth Sciences* (Cambridge: At the University Press, 1981), p. 381.

30. Stanley, *New Evolutionary Timetable*, p. 114.

31. Eldredge, p. 146.

32. K. J. Hsu, *The Great Dying* (New York: Harcourt Brace Jovanovich, 1986), p. 88.

33. Ibid., p. 281.

34. S. J. Gould, in *Conceptual Issues in Evolutionary Biology*, edited by E. Sober, (Cambridge, Mass.: MIT Press, 1984), pp. 256, 260.

35. Stanley, *New Evolutionary Timetable*, p. 153.

36. Ibid., p. 151.

37. Ibid.

38. E. Trinkhaus and W. W. Howells, *Scientific American*, vol. 241, December 1979, pp. 94–105.

39. The hominids comprise the extinct genus *Australopithecus* and the present-day genus *Homo*, of which Modern Man is the only living species. Regarding *Australopithecus*, the recent discovery (A. Walker et al., *Nature*, vol. 322, August 1986, pp. 517–522) of Skull KNM-WT 17000 (the "Black Skull") has confounded the evolutionists. This fossil has cast serious doubts on the previously held notion of straight-line australopithecine evolution with well-defined transitional forms. Indeed, the Black Skull has become the source of a spirited dispute between Professor Alan Walker (and colleagues) and Professor Donald Johanson (and colleagues). The present arguments are quite reminiscent of the sharp debate of the middle 1970s between Johanson and Leakey regarding *Australopithecus afarensis*, the famous fossil nicknamed "Lucy." Johanson's discovery of this fossil in 1974 invalidated the previously accepted Leakey proposal for the "family tree" of man.

Current understanding is equally lacking for the early species of the genus *Homo* (see Appendix B). The recent discovery (D. C. Johanson et al., *Nature*, vol. 327, May 1987, pp. 205–209) of hominid specimen OH-62 has again confounded the evolutionary biologists. This fossil makes unclear the place of *Homo habilis* (the earliest species of *Homo*) in the "family tree" of man. For a discussion of the important implications of this hominid specimen, see below n. 40.

40. B. Wood, *Nature*, vol. 327, May 1987, pp. 187–188.

The Fifth Day (Part II)
The Origin of Life

[20]*And God said, "Let the waters swarm with living creatures, and let winged creatures fly above the earth across the firmament of the heaven."* [21]*And God created the large sea-creatures and every living creature that crawls, with which the waters swarmed, after its kind, and every winged creature after its kind. And God saw that it was good.* [22]*And God blessed them, saying, "Be fruitful and multiply, and fill the waters in the seas, and let the winged creatures proliferate on land."* [23]*And there was evening and there was morning—a fifth day.*

QUESTIONS

The fifth day of creation deals with the initial stages of the animal kingdom. A question that is often asked regarding the origin of life relates to an apparent contradiction between the biblical text and recent scientific evidence. The question is commonly phrased in the following way:

The past few decades have witnessed an enormous increase in our knowledge of molecular biology. The genetic code has been deciphered. The complex mechanism by which proteins are formed is now understood. Furthermore, it has been demonstrated that all the basic molecules necessary for life could have formed gradually from simple chemicals that exist in nature. Moreover, scientists have recently succeeded in explaining all the steps that took place during the gradual evolution of inanimate matter into the complex biological systems that we call life. Therefore, from the scientific perspective, the riddle of the origin of life has now been solved.

In complete contrast to the scientific view, we read in verse 1:21 that living organisms appeared suddenly, as the result of a divine act of creation. Therefore, the biblical text is incompatible with the scientific notion that life originated gradually from simple chemicals.

In this chapter, we shall show that the popular view outlined above is incorrect on three basic counts. First, the current fossil evidence indicates that living organisms appeared *suddenly*, with no sign at all of a "gradual evolution of life." Secondly, recent advances in molecular biology have revealed a seemingly insurmountable difficulty that confronts every proposed scientific theory of the origin of life. Thirdly, a careful reading of the biblical text shows that there is, in fact, no inconsistency with the notion that living organisms were formed from inanimate matter. We shall now discuss each of these three points.

THE FIRST LIVING ORGANISMS

When the earth was first formed, its temperature was so high that the planet was molten.[1] Only later did the surface of the earth cool sufficiently for rocks to solidify. Geologists have discovered some of the oldest rocks on earth in places as diverse as Greenland, Western Australia, and Swaziland in southern Africa.

When did the first living organisms appear? It had previously been widely believed that life evolved gradually in the course of billions of years. Recent fossil evidence has caused this view to be discarded. "Perhaps the most striking aspect [of the first appearance] of life on earth is that it happened so fast. . . . The step to life seems to have been easier than one might have expected."[2]

This new understanding has emerged from the study of ancient rocks. "Since the 1950s, it has come to be recognized that . . . fossils [of living organisms] can be found even in some of the most ancient sedimentary deposits known."[3] The second oldest known rocks (from Western Australia) show "unequivocal remains of life."[4] This conclusion derives from "the geological and the paleontological evidence which suggest that [this Australian rock formation] was indeed the habitat of some of the earth's earliest living things."[5] Moreover, the oldest known rocks (from Isua in Greenland) show "a common manifestation of biospheric activity. It would be consistent with such evidence [but not conclusive] to postulate the presence of life even that early."[6]

The current fossil data thus contradict the notion of the "gradual evolution of life." The ancient rocks containing the fossils of the earliest living organisms date back almost to the time that the surface of the earth solidified. This supports the idea that the first living organisms appeared *suddenly*, almost as soon as the earth had cooled sufficiently to enable life to exist.

NUCLEIC ACIDS AND PROTEINS

The basic unit of all living organisms is the cell. The most important molecules in the living cell are the proteins and the nucleic acids.[7] For our discussion of the origin of life, it is necessary to describe very briefly some of the basic properties of these two types of molecules.

One of the characteristic features of a living organism is its ability to reproduce itself. Living creatures reproduce, whereas inanimate objects do not.[8] The reproduction of the organism depends, ultimately, on the reproduction of the individual cell. This is called cellular replication. The mechanism for cellular replication is identical in all living organisms. It is based on the unique properties of the nucleic acids known as DNA and RNA. (The older scientific literature spoke of chromosomes, which are now known to be extremely long strands of the nucleic acid DNA; a gene is a segment of a chromosome.) A molecule of nucleic acid replicates by producing two identical daughter molecules from the original parent molecule. Furthermore, nucleic acids control the production of all the proteins in the cell. In this way, nucleic acids cause the cell to replicate. The complex processes that take place during cellular replication are now well understood.

A major component of the living cell is a group of large molecules called proteins. They make up about 70–80 percent of the dry weight of a typical cell. A living cell contains hundreds of different types of proteins, with each type carrying out a specialized task needed for the cell to function as a living entity. The proteins catalyze the chemical reactions that take place in the cell, control cellular metabolism, and "manufacture" many cellular "products." In brief, they regulate and control almost every activity that occurs in the cell. It would be quite impossible for any living cell to exist without proteins.

Where do proteins come from? *All proteins are produced by the nucleic acids.* No other mechanism exists for producing proteins. This assertion is known as the "central dogma of molecular biology."

What regulates the replication of nucleic acids? *The replication of nucleic acids can take place only in the presence of certain proteins called enzymes.* Indeed, without enzymes, nucleic acids could not exist at all. The large nucleic-acid molecules would decompose in the water of the cell (all living cells contain water) were it not for the stabilizing effect of the proteins.

THE PARADOX OF THE ORIGIN OF LIFE

The discussion in the previous section provides the necessary background for a critical analysis of the proposal that life generated itself from inanimate matter. There are four points to the argument.

1. All living cells require nucleic acids for replication. Therefore, without nucleic acids, there can be no life.
2. All living cells require proteins to carry out the many activities needed to maintain the cell. Therefore, without proteins, there can be no life.
3. Proteins are produced *only* by nucleic acids. Therefore, without nucleic acids, there can be no proteins.
4. Nucleic acids are able to replicate *only* in the presence of proteins. Therefore, without proteins, there can be no nucleic acids.

The paradox regarding the spontaneous origin of life can now be easily stated. Points (1) and (2) imply that living cells need *both* proteins *and* nucleic acids. Points (3) and (4) imply that neither of these complex molecules can be produced without the other. Therefore, it follows that life *could not* have developed from inanimate matter because inanimate matter contains *neither* proteins *nor* nucleic acids.

This paradox is well known to biologists, who often compare it to the riddle of "which came first, the chicken or the egg?" The analogy is clear. A few quotations will illustrate the point.

> Nucleic acids could not replicate or direct protein synthesis without the help of preformed proteins; no proteins could be synthesized without the information stored in preformed nucleic acids. One of our major problems is to see how such a "hen-and-egg" situation could have developed.[9]

> This, then, is still a point of debate among origin-of-life theorists: which came first, not the chicken or the egg, but nucleic acids or proteins? Right now, no one really knows.[10]

> One of the many critical unresolved problems in understanding the origin of life is the first functional relation between proteins and nucleic acids—did proteins or nucleic acids occur first?[11]

This final stage [in the origin of life] still remains totally incomprehensible, which explains why it has become the focus of intensive laboratory research.[12]

Nucleic acids cannot replicate without enzymes [proteins], and enzymes cannot be made without nucleic acids.[13]

A marvelous illustration of this "chicken-and-egg" paradox regarding the origin of life has been given by Professor Frank Shu of the University of California, in terms of the famous lithograph *Drawing Hands* by M. C. Escher.[14] This illustration is reproduced below.

Finally, we mention the recent proposal of Professor Graham Cairns-Smith of the University of Glasgow. Professor Cairns-Smith is convinced that the paradox regarding the origin of life has *no* resolution. Therefore, he rejects the notion that life *as we*

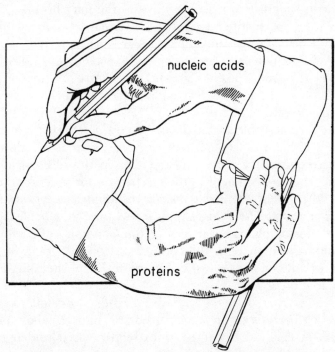

Adaptation of lithograph *Drawing Hands* by M. C. Escher illustrates the paradox of the origin of life. Let one hand represent nucleic acids, and the other hand represent proteins. Which came first, nucleic acids or proteins?

know it could possibly have arisen naturally because "one of the places where proteins are most needed is in the machinery for making proteins."[15] He suggests instead that one should consider life as we do *not* know it, to which the paradox may not apply. His specific proposal is that the first organisms "may have been crystals of clay."[16]

In view of the preceding discussion, it is quite clear that there exists no accepted scientific explanation for the origin of life from inanimate matter.

'EVOLUTION'

We have seen that the earliest living cells first appeared on the earth almost as soon as the surface of the planet had cooled sufficiently for life to exist. In view of the long history of the earth, it had been anticipated that the fundamental mechanisms that take place in the cell would have gradually evolved over the years. To explore this question, biologists have studied the changes that have taken place in the course of time in the mechanisms whereby nucleic acids replicate and whereby proteins are produced.

It is a remarkable fact that essentially *no changes* have been found in either mechanism. In other words, there is *no* indication of any evolutionary development either in the mechanism for nucleic-acid replication or in the mechanism for protein production. *Both of these exceedingly complex mechanisms were found to be already present and fully developed in the earliest known living organisms.* Professor Hyman Hartman of the University of California has emphasized that "in the speculations on the origin of life, the most difficult conceptual problems deal with the complexity of the first organism."[17]

The spectrum of living organisms ranges from microscopic one-celled bacteria to the large vertebrate animals, whose many billions of cells are organized into highly specialized organs. Bacteria are the earth's oldest organisms, whereas the mammals arrived relatively recently. Therefore, by comparing the nucleic acids and proteins of, say, bacteria with those of mammals, one can study any evolutionary development that might have occurred in the past.[18]

Detailed studies have revealed that the mechanisms for nu-cleic-acid replication and for protein production are *the same* in all living organisms, with no sign of any gradual evolutionary development. From the simplest bacterium to the most complex mammal, *all* living cells contain the same two nucleic acids (DNA and RNA). And in *all* species, the nucleic acids replicate and proteins are produced in precisely *the same way*. This universality is known as the "unity of biochemistry". Professor Graham Cairns-Smith explains:

> A curious similarity underlies the seemingly varied forms of life we see on earth today: the most central molecular machinery of modern organisms has always been found to be essentially the same. This unity of biochemistry has surely been one of the great discoveries of the past 100 years.[19]

THE BIBLICAL TEXT

In the biblical account of the formation of the animal king-dom, we read that "God created" the first animals (1:21). In this context, the verb "create" need not be understood in the physical sense ("something out of nothing"). Creation implies the forma-tion of something *fundamentally new*—either physically new (as in creation *ex nihilo*) or conceptually new. A living organism surely qualifies as an entity that is conceptually new when compared with inanimate matter.

The foregoing discussion suggests that in reference to the first animals, the biblical expression "God created" denotes the trans-formation of inanimate matter into living organisms. Indeed, this divinely directed transformation resulted in an entity whose properties are so utterly different from the original inanimate matter that no verb other than "created" seems adequate to describe the change.

This interpretation of the biblical text is consistent with the views of many traditional Jewish biblical commentators. In fact, in his comment on Genesis 1:21–25, Malbim presents *precisely* this analysis of the word "created". Similarly, both Radak (David Kimchi) and Ramban (Moses Nachmanides) explain that the words "God created" refer *only* to the act of imparting life to the animals, in contrast to the physical component of the animals, which was derived from inanimate materials. Therefore, there is no inconsistency at all between the notion that living organisms originated from inanimate matter and the biblical account of the appearance of the first animals.

AN "ACCIDENTAL OCCURRENCE"

No discussion of life should conclude without mentioning that the very existence of living organisms on this planet is due to a remarkable "accidental occurrence." Life on earth depends on the sun, whose heat and light are the primary source of all terrestrial energy. Without the sun, there would not even be an earth, much less a planet capable of supporting life. Therefore, we shall examine briefly the mechanism that produces the sun's energy.

Two of the most important particles in nature are the proton and the neutron. When the sun was first formed, it consisted primarily of protons. Because of the special conditions present in the sun, a proton is occasionally transformed into a neutron (plus other particles that need not concern us here). The resulting neutron can combine with another proton to form the composite particle known as a deuteron. The deuterons that are present in the sun "burn" to produce a thermonuclear reaction. The thermonuclear reaction that takes place in the sun is the source of its intense heat. And the heat energy of the sun enables life to exist on earth.

In order to understand the conditions necessary for the occurrence of a thermonuclear reaction in the sun, let us consider the analogy of a bonfire. A bonfire produces heat energy as long as it continues to burn. However, burning requires fuel—usually wood—as well as a means for igniting the fuel. The wood of a bonfire may be ignited by using a little kerosene or some paper or simply by lighting a match. After the wood catches fire, it becomes the primary source of the heat of the bonfire, and the ignition material—kerosene or paper—is no longer important. On the other hand, if the wood fails to ignite, the ignition material quickly burns up and the bonfire goes out.

In the sun, the deuterons serve as the fuel, and gravitational energy served as the means for initially· "igniting" this fuel. Therefore, the thermonuclear reaction ("burning") will continue as long as there is an adequate supply of deuterons. However, there was another requirement that had to be met for thermonuclear reactions to take place in the sun. A proton must be *unable* to combine with another proton. If protons could combine with each other, the result would be an "explosion" which would totally prevent the gradual "burning" of the deuterons. One may compare this situation to a bonfire whose fuel consists of dynamite, instead of wood. Igniting such a bonfire would immediately lead to a violent explosion, without any gradual burning whatsoever.

In summary, for thermonuclear reactions to take place in the sun, two conditions must be met. First, a proton must be *able* to combine with a neutron to form a deuteron (fuel must be *present*). Secondly, a proton must be *unable* to combine with another proton (explosive material must be *absent*). The possibility of proton-neutron combination and the possibility of proton-proton combination *both* depend on the strength of the nuclear force. Detailed calculations of the nuclear force have led to the following results:[20]

1. If the nuclear force were only a *few percent* weaker, then a proton would *not* combine with a neutron to form a deuteron. If this were the case, there would be no deuterons present in the sun and hence no fuel for the sun's thermonuclear reaction.[21] As a result, the sun's "ignition energy" would soon be used up and the sun would quickly cease to shine.

2. If the nuclear force were only a *few percent* stronger, then a proton *would* combine with another proton. If this were the case, then all the protons in the sun would combine with each other with explosive results, just as a bonfire containing dynamite would explode. Once again, there would soon be nothing left to "burn" in the sun and, once again, the sun would quickly cease to shine.

It is extraordinary that the nuclear force *just happens* to lie in the narrow range in which *neither* of these two catastrophes occurs. Therefore, thermonuclear reactions *do* take place in the sun, providing the warmth and light that are vital for life to exist on our planet.

Many scientists have commented on this "accidental occurrence." Professor Freeman J. Dyson of the Institute for Advanced Study in Princeton has remarked that "nature has been kinder to us than we had any right to expect."[22] Similarly, Professor M. J. Rees of the University of Cambridge has noted that "the possibility of life as we know it depends on the values of a few basic physical constants and is, in some respects, remarkably sensitive to their numerical values . . . nature does exhibit remarkable coincidences."[23]

The thermonuclear reaction that causes the sun to shine and thus to warm the earth may be added to the long list of "accidental occurrences" that are necessary for the existence and well-being of man—and just happen to occur. The secular scientist expresses surprise at so many "accidental occurrences." However, the astonishment quickly disappears if one sees divine purpose, instead of arbitrariness, in the laws of nature.

NOTES

1. D. G. Smith, chief ed., *The Cambridge Encyclopedia of Earth Sciences* (Cambridge: At the University Press, 1981), p. 260.

2. R. E. Dickerson, *Scientific American*, vol. 239, September 1978, p. 62.

3. J. W. Schopf, *Scientific American*, vol. 239, September 1978, p. 86.

4. Smith, p. 357.

5. D. I. Groves et al., *Scientific American*, vol. 245, October 1981, p. 56.

6. P. Cloud, *Scientific American*, vol. 249, September 1983, p. 137.

7. There exist organisms which biologists classify as borderline between living and nonliving. These are the viruses and the viroids, which have been shown to be the cause of many diseases in both plants and animals. Viruses and viroids have no cell structure. Therefore, by themselves, they are *unable* to reproduce, the fundamental property of a living organism. However, when they invade a living cell, they take over the reproductive machinery of the host cell and harness it to the task of making more viruses and viroids, usually killing the cell in the process. Even though viruses have no cell structure, they are nevertheless composed of proteins and nucleic acids.

8. The reader might object to this definition on the grounds that it excludes mules and seedless grapes, which do *not* reproduce but most certainly *are* alive. This objection is easily overcome by generalizing the definition slightly to include all creatures that *either* reproduce *or* are the offspring of a creature that reproduces.

9. L. E. Orgel, *The Origins of Life* (London: Chapman & Hall, 1973), p. 49.

10. F. H. Shu, *The Physical Universe* (Mill Valley, Calif.: University Science Books, 1982), p. 533.

11. Smith, p. 352.

12. J. Audouze et al., eds., *The Cambridge Atlas of Astronomy* (Cambridge: At the University Press, 1985), p. 389.

13. Dickerson, p. 65.

14. Shu, p. 534.

15. A. G. Cairns-Smith, *Scientific American*, vol. 252, June 1985, p. 74.

16. Ibid.

17. H. Hartman, *Journal of Molecular Evolution*, vol. 4, 1975, p. 359.

18. This is also the basis of the so-called "protein clock" or the "molecular clock" for DNA. The data derived from this "clock" help establish the past history and relationships between contemporary animals.

19. Cairns-Smith, p. 74.

20. P. C. W. Davies, *Journal of Physics*, vol. 5, 1972, pp. 1296–1304.

21. Strictly speaking, there exists another type of thermonuclear reaction, called the carbon-nitrogen cycle reaction, which does not depend on the presence of deuterons. However, this alternate type of thermonuclear reaction occurs only in much hotter stars, so hot that life could not have formed. A

discussion of this point can be found in *Scientific American* (December 1981, pp. 114–122).

22. F. J. Dyson, *Scientific American*, vol. 225, September 1971, p. 59.

23. B. J. Carr and M. J. Rees, *Nature*, vol. 278, March 1979, p. 612.

The Fifth Day (Part III)
The Animal Kingdom

GENESIS—CHAPTER I

²⁰*And God said, "Let the waters swarm with living creatures, and let winged creatures fly above the earth across the firmament of the heaven." ²¹And God created the large sea-creatures and every living creature that crawls, with which the waters swarmed, after its kind, and every winged creature after its kind. And God saw that it was good. ²²And God blessed them, saying, "Be fruitful and multiply, and fill the waters in the seas, and let the winged creatures proliferate on land." ²³And there was evening and there was morning—a fifth day.*

²⁴*And God said, "Let the earth bring forth the living creature after its kind: cattle, and the crawling creature, and the beast of the land after its kind." And it was so. ²⁵And God made the beast of the land after its kind, and the cattle after its kind, and every creature that crawls on the ground after its kind. And God saw that it was good.*

QUESTIONS

The fifth day and the beginning of the sixth day of creation deal with the formation of the animals, as described in Genesis 1:20–25. The biblical text raises the following questions.

1. We read that the first animals to be formed were "the large sea-creatures" (Hebrew *tanninim*) (1:21).[1] In fact, it is well known that the first animals were tiny marine organisms, and only very much later did any large sea-creatures appear. Moreover, these "large sea-creatures" are not mentioned in any of the subsequent biblical verses. What rational meaning could one possibly attribute to such mysterious creatures?

2. We read the divine pronouncement: "Let the waters swarm with living creatures" (1:20). In fact, it is well known that animal life evolved very gradually over long periods of time. Indeed, the very notion that the seas suddenly became filled with vast numbers of marine animals of all kinds borders on mythology.

3. Why was the formation of the animals divided between *two* separate days of creation? Why do some animals (marine and winged species) appear on the fifth day (1:20–23), whereas other animals (terrestrial species) do not appear until the sixth day (1:24–25)? It is surprising that the formation of the animal kingdom was not completed on a single day of creation.

4. The formation of "every winged creature" is associated with the fifth day of creation (1:21). However, the birds first appeared at about the same time as the mammals. Therefore, why is the formation of the birds not associated with the sixth day, together with the mammals?

We shall now present the recent fossil evidence which provides an explanation of the biblical text that is consistent with current scientific knowledge.

ANIMALS OF THE CAMBRIAN PERIOD

Geologists of the last century divided the history of the earth into major divisions according to the dominant form of animal life in each era. The time interval corresponding to the oldest known fossils was named the Paleozoic era (from *paleo* meaning "ancient" and *zoic* meaning "life"). The Paleozoic era was subdivided into periods (see Appendix A), the earliest being the Cambrian period, in which it was thought that animal life began.

In contrast to the popular view, the paleontological (fossil) evidence from the Cambrian period shows *no sign* of the gradual evolution of animal life. Quite the contrary. To the surprise of the paleontologists, the Cambrian fossil record shows the *sudden* appearance of a vast profusion of animals. The data are so striking that the dramatic proliferation of animal life is emphasized in every scientific account of the Cambrian period. A few quotations will illustrate the point.

> Perhaps the most astonishing aspect of the Cambrian fauna is that so many radically different types of animals appeared in such a short interval. . . . The Cambrian Period saw the appearance of new phyla and classes [of animals] at a rate that has not been matched since.[2]

> The Cambrian Period ushered in an explosion of multicellular lifeforms . . . the explosion of lifeforms which inaugurated the Cambrian Period.[3]

> A hypothetical observer in the late Precambrian [Period] would have had few grounds for optimism about the future of life. Yet, over a comparatively short period . . . the initial diversification of metazoans [animals] gave way to a series of dazzling radiations during the Cambrian Period. . . . Paleontologists are impressed by the rapidity of the development of such a diverse range of organisms (ten or more invertebrate phyla).[4]

> A tremendous explosion of life took place in the Cambrian Period. The start of the Cambrian Period marks the first appearance of a large number of major groups of animals. . . . The sudden appearance of animal fossils in the lowest [earliest] Cambrian strata, and the absence of fossils in Precambrian strata, made the boundary between Precambrian and Cambrian Periods the cardinal division of the geological time scale.[5]

Scientists have long sought to understand—without much success—this "explosion of lifeforms," characterized by the "sudden appearance" and "dazzling radiation" of so many different types of animals, all dating from the same time, the beginning of the Cambrian period. While the paleontologists "continue to search for triggering mechanisms,"[6] it is generally conceded that "it remains unsettled exactly how the metazoans [animals] arose."[7]

THE FIRST ANIMALS

In addition to not understanding the causes of the Cambrian explosion of lifeforms, paleontologists have also been perplexed by another question: "Where were the ancestral forms that had given rise to these plentiful, advanced and diverse [Cambrian] sea animals?"[8] Recent fossil evidence regarding this question has led to a number of additional surprises.

Fossils of extinct animals traditionally consist of bones or shells or imprints in rocks. Soft-bodied sea creatures do not usually leave such tangible signs of their existence. However, improved techniques have recently enabled paleontologists to discover very ancient fossils that had previously escaped detection. As a result, fossils of soft-bodied marine creatures that predate the earliest Cambrian animals have been discovered during the last few years. In fact, in many areas throughout the world, "well-documented Precambrian fauna have been described."[9] Detailed studies have shown these fauna to be "a remarkable and diverse group of soft-bodied aquatic animals, the first known metazoans [animals]."[10] These earliest animals are called the Ediacaran fauna, after the Ediacara Hills of South Australia, where the first specimens were discovered.

These recent fossil discoveries have shown that the Ediacaran fauna existed in vast abundance. Indeed, the extent of their proliferation has taken paleontologists by surprise. "A major enigma is the abundance and widespread distribution of the Ediacaran fauna."[11]

Most astonishing was the great size of the Precambrian Ediacaran fauna, which include creatures that are "gigantic by Cambrian standards."[12] Contrary to all expectations, these first animals "are scarcely the kind of near-microscopic forms that many paleontologists had expected to find at the base of the metazoan [animal] lineage."[13]

Another characteristic feature of the Ediacaran fauna is their extremely strange appearance. These bizarre creatures bear no resemblance to the animal kingdom of today. Rather, it is the subsequent Cambrian lifeforms that provide the basis for the present-day panorama of animal life. "Modern animals are the direct decendants of the animals that first appeared during the Cambrian explosion."[14]

What happened to these peculiar Ediacaran fauna? The fossil record shows that they became extinct shortly after they first appeared. The beginning of the Cambrian period "saw the disappearance of the Ediacaran fauna."[15]

In summary, the Ediacaran fauna remain a mystery. These first animals appeared suddenly, proliferated rapidly throughout the world, and then suddenly disappeared. Most were so unusual in form that they clearly did not serve as the antecedents of the contemporary animal kingdom. Present-day animal life began only later with the profuse Cambrian proliferation. Indeed, there is a tendency among biologists to dismiss the enigmatic Ediacaran fauna as an anomaly in the general biological scheme, referring to them, "with the benefit of hindsight, as a short-lived experiment."[16]

THE INSECTS, THE MAMMALS, THE BIRDS, AND THE REPTILES

The animal kingdom is divided into more than twenty large groups called phyla (singular: phylum), and each phylum is divided into a number of classes. The mammals, birds, and reptiles are three different classes that belong to the same phylum (which also includes fish and amphibians); the insects are a class that belongs to a different phylum (which also includes spiders and crabs).

Insects are by far the most numerous class in the entire animal kingdom, comprising about half of all animal species. Insects first appeared in the middle of the Paleozoic era. Their unique feature was their ability to fly. Indeed, for a very long time, insects were the *only* flying creatures. During the latter half of the Paleozoic era, "the insects dominated the air unchallenged by any other winged form—reptile, bird or mammal."[17] In past ages, insects included gigantic species. "The fossil of one primitive dragonfly shows a wing span of 30 inches [nearly 80 centi-meters]."[18] The Paleozoic sky was filled with an enormous variety of huge insects foraging for food. The insects were so important that this time is often referred to as the Age of Insects.

The animals whose natural habitat is the dry land vary greatly in size. Of particular importance are the large land animals—mammals, reptiles, and birds. In the Mesozoic era (see Appendix A), the most important animals were huge reptiles (the dino-saurs) who dominated to such an extent that this time is often called the Age of Reptiles. Similarly, mammals are the dominant animals in the contemporary Cenozoic era, which is therefore called the Age of Mammals.

The most striking difference between the class of insects and the classes of large land animals is the enormous disparity between the number of species in each class. Biologists have identified about 4000 species of mammals, 9000 of birds, and 6000 of reptiles (crocodiles, snakes, lizards, and turtles). In complete contrast to these numbers, *nearly one million* different species of insects have thus far been identified.

It should be emphasized that the insects did *not* evolve gradu-ally. The fossil evidence indicates that "the first insects multi-plied and diversified . . . in a population explosion of unmatched size."[19] This illustrates once again that the Darwinian concept of the gradual evolution of species is contradicted by current fossil evidence.

THE BIBLICAL TEXT

Having described some of the most important events in the development of the animal kingdom, we are in a position to make a comparison between the biblical text and current scientific knowledge. We shall relate to the questions that were posed at the beginning of this chapter.

1. The fossil record shows that the earliest animals were surprisingly large aquatic creatures ("gigantic by Cambrian standards"[20]), called the Ediacaran fauna. The biblical statement that the first animals were "large sea-creatures" (1:21) may there-fore be understood as referring to the Ediacaran fauna.

The Ediacaran fauna appeared in "abundance and widespread distribution."[21] However, they were extremely strange animals that were *not* the antecedents of the present-day animal kingdom. Moreover, for unknown reasons, these creatures became extinct shortly after their appearance, and are therefore sometimes characterized as "a short-lived experiment."[22]

All these features of the Ediacaran fauna are consistent with the biblical account of the "large sea-creatures" *(tanninim)*. After their formation, the "large sea-creatures" are not mentioned in any of the subsequent verses, nor are they associated with present-day animals in any biblical passage. In fact, Rashi, the most famous of Jewish biblical commentators, points out in his discussion of Genesis 1:21, that the "large sea-creatures" were destroyed shortly after their formation.

2. Even more striking is the correspondence between the scientific evidence and the remainder of verse 1:21. After referring to the "large sea-creatures," the text specifies the next step in the formation of the animals, stating that "the waters swarmed" with animal life. This may be understood as referring to the dramatic events that occurred at the beginning of the Cambrian period, immediately following the Precambrian Ediacaran fauna. Every scientific account of marine life in the Cambrian period emphasizes the astonishing "explosion of life-forms,"[23] featuring the "sudden appearance"[24] and "dazzling radiation"[25] of "new phyla and classes [of marine animals] at a rate that has not been matched since."[26]

Scientists have not found any explanation for the sudden appearance of so many different kinds of marine animals which inaugurated the contemporary animal kingdom, and they "continue to search for triggering mechanisms."[27] In contrast to the scientist, the Book of Genesis *does* give an explanation for the "triggering mechanisms"—an explanation that is written in verse 1:20: "And God said, 'Let the waters swarm' . . ."

The third step in the development of the animal kingdom, as given in verse 1:21, was the formation of "every winged creature." The biblical commentator Radak emphasizes that the phrase "every winged creature" refers to *all* winged creatures, including the *insects* (almost all insects have wings) as well as the birds.[28] This explicit biblical reference to the formation of the insects is completely consistent with the scientific evidence, which has established that the appearance of insects constituted a major step in the development of the animal kingdom. Insects were not only the first flying creatures, they were also among the earliest and most important colonizers of the land. They produced ecological changes that paved the way for all subsequent terrestrial animals. Therefore, it is certainly to be expected that the biblical account of the formation of the animal kingdom would mention the all-important insects.

3. The development of the animal kingdom occurred in two stages. The first stage ended with the close of the Paleozoic era, and featured the appearance of marine animals and the insects. This stage was distinguished by two dramatic population explosions in which marine life and later the insects appeared suddenly and in vast abundance. The second stage in the formation of the animals took place after the Paleozoic era, and featured the colonization of the land by large terrestrial species. The dominant animals were huge reptiles and mammals. During this second stage, no population explosion of any sort occurred. Because of the striking differences between the dominant animal life in each of the two stages, geologists refer to them as different eras.

Just as the scientific account of the development of the animal kingdom can be divided into two distinct stages, the biblical account is also divided into two distinct stages, each stage being associated with a different day of creation. The two biblical stages of the development of animals *exactly* parallel the two stages implied by the fossil record, as will now be shown.

On the fifth day of creation—the first stage—those animals are mentioned that appeared *before* the end of the Paleozoic era ("large sea-creatures," marine animals and insects). Moreover, the Book of Genesis states that God blessed the animals formed on the fifth day of creation, enjoining them "to be fruitful and multiply" (1:22)—the marine animals "to fill the waters in the seas," and the winged creatures "to proliferate on land." The fulfillment of the divine will is recorded in the fossils. Scientific accounts of the fossil data invariably comment, often in utter astonishment, on the enormous proliferation of the early marine animals ("the Cambrian explosion of lifeforms"[29]) and of the insects ("a population explosion of unmatched size"[30]). Even though destined for early extinction, the Ediacaran fauna ("the large sea-creatures") also spread quickly over the entire planet ("abundance and widespread distribution").[31]

On the sixth day of creation—the second stage—those animals are mentioned that appeared *after* the Paleozoic era (mammals and other terrestrial species). Moreover, these animals were *not* specially enjoined by God "to proliferate." Correspondingly, no population explosion of these animals ever took place. In striking contrast to the nearly *one million* different species of insects (fifth day of creation—proliferation), there are *only four thousand* species of mammals (sixth day of creation—no proliferation). Similarly, *ten different phyla* of marine animals (fifth day) appeared suddenly in the Cambrian explosion, whereas all the large terrestrial animals (sixth day) belong to a *single phylum*.

4. The preceding discussion makes it possible to explain the biblical account of the formation of the birds. If the expression "every winged creature" (1:21) referred *only* to birds, then these words should properly have appeared in the account of the sixth day of creation. This would have been appropriate because both birds and mammals first appeared at about the same time, *after* the Paleozoic era. Thus, both groups of animals belong to the second stage in the development of the animal kingdom, which is associated with the sixth day of creation.

However, the expression "every winged creature" *also* refers to insects. The insects date from *before* the end of the Paleozoic era and thus belong to the *first* stage of animal development. For this reason, the general expression "every winged creature" appears in the account of the fifth day of creation.

NOTES

1. Specific guidance is lacking regarding the etymology of the Hebrew word *tanninim*. The traditional translation of "sea-creatures" follows the biblical commentator Rashi (see his comments on verse 1:21). This translation is also suggested by a comparison between verses 1:20 and 1:21. For a more complete discussion, see E. Munk, *The Seven Days of the Beginning* (Jerusalem: Feldheim, 1974), pp. 77–79. In his book, Munk presents a comprehensive analysis of biblical etymology relevant to the first chapter of the Book of Genesis.

2. M. A. S. McMenamin, *Scientific American*, vol. 256, April 1987, p. 90.

3. F. H. Shu, *The Physical Universe* (Mill Valley, Calif.: University Science Books, 1982), pp. 503, 545.

4. D. G. Smith, chief ed., *The Cambridge Encyclopedia of Earth Sciences* (Cambridge: At the University Press, 1981), pp. 370–371.

5. McMenamin, p. 84.

6. Smith, p. 371.

7. P. Cloud, *Scientific American*, vol. 249, September 1983, p. 143.

8. McMenamin, p. 84.

9. Smith, p. 370.

10. Cloud, p. 135. Animals are often referred to as metazoans in the scientific literature, after their Latin name: Kingdom Metazoa.

11. Smith, p. 371.

12. McMenamin, p. 91.

13. Cloud, p. 144.

14. McMenamin, p. 92.

15. Ibid., p. 84.

16. Ibid.

17. P. Farb, *The Insects* (New York: Time Books, 1972), p. 18.

18. Ibid., p. 12.

19. Ibid., p. 17. The enormity of the number of different *species* of insects, combined with the amazing rapidity with which they appeared, is the source of the expression "population explosion of unmatched size." It should be noted that this explosion is of a different nature from the Cambrian explosion of lifeforms, which refers to the large number of new *phyla and classes* of marine animals that appeared so suddenly at the beginning of the Paleozoic era.

20. McMenamin, p. 91.

21. Smith, p. 371.

22. McMenamin, p. 84.

23. Shu, p. 503.

24. McMenamin, p. 84.

25. Smith, p. 370.

26. McMenamin, p. 90.

27. Smith, p. 371.

28. Radak makes these comments on the same words in verse 7:14. Rashi and other commentators make a similar statement regarding these words in verse 7:14, but Radak is most explicit. This important point has been noted by E. Munk, *The Seven Days of the Beginning* (Jerusalem: Feldheim, 1974), p. 79.

29. Shu, p. 503.

30. Farb, p. 17.

31. Smith, p. 371.

The Sixth Day (Part I)
The Uniqueness of Man

GENESIS—CHAPTER I

²⁴*And God said, "Let the earth bring forth the living creature after its kind: cattle, and the crawling creature, and the beast of the land after its kind." And it was so.* ²⁵*And God made the beast of the land after its kind, and the cattle after its kind, and every creature that crawls on the ground after its kind. And God saw that it was good.* ²⁶*And God said, "Let us make man in our image, after our likeness. And they shall rule over the fish of the sea, and over the winged creatures of the air, and over the cattle, and over the entire earth, and over every crawling creature that crawls upon the earth."* ²⁷*And God created man in His image; in the image of God, He created him; male and female He created them.* ²⁸*And God blessed them and God said to them, "Be fruitful and multiply, and fill the land and subdue it; and rule over the fish of the sea, and over the winged creatures of the air, and over every living creature that crawls upon the earth."* ²⁹*And God said, "Behold, I have given you every herb yielding seed which is on all the land, and every tree which has fruit bearing seed; for you it shall be for food.* ³⁰*And for every beast of the land, and for every winged creature of the air, and for everything that crawls upon the earth which has life within it, every green herb is for food." And it was so.* ³¹*And God saw everything that He had made, and behold, it was very good. And there was evening and there was morning— the sixth day.*

QUESTIONS

The sixth day of creation deals with man, as described in Genesis 1:26–31. The biblical text raises several questions.

1. We read that "God created man . . . in the image of God" (1:27), clearly implying that man is unique among living creatures. The notion that the human species is somehow unique is utterly without scientific foundation. As is well known, extensive fossil evidence has yielded the evolutionary history of the human species, extending back millions of years to primitive apelike creatures. The claim that man was "created" only a few thousand years ago is mere folklore.

2. We read that "God blessed them [Adam and Eve]," telling them to "fill the land and subdue it" (1:28). Needless to say, there is no archaeological evidence whatsoever to support the idea that man suddenly "filled the land and subdued it." Therefore, what meaning can one attribute to this blessing?

We shall now present scientific evidence that provides an explanation of the biblical text that is consistent with current scientific knowledge.

"GRADUAL EVOLUTION" AND MAN

The hominids—the family of "man-like" species—include only one living species. This is contemporary Modern Man, whose scientific designation is *Homo sapiens sapiens*. Anthropologists once believed in the so-called single-species hypothesis. According to this hypothesis, the most primitive hominid species gradually evolved into a somewhat more advanced species, which in turn gradually evolved into a still more advanced species, and so on. The process was repeated several times, until it resulted in the most advanced hominid species of all—Modern Man. Each new hominid species that was discovered was interpreted as representing one more phase in the straight-line evolutionary development from the earliest ape-like species to Modern Man.

The single-species hypothesis has been discarded on the basis of recent fossil evidence. Professor Niles Eldredge, Curator at the American Museum of Natural History, refers to this hypothesis as "the great evolutionary myth of slow, gradual and progressive change. So bewitched were the single-species people by the linear elegance of this myth that they were reluctant to see it marred."[1] Emphasizing that the current fossil data completely contradict the Darwinian concept of gradualism, Professor Eldredge notes: "Our standard expectation of evolution—slow, steady, gradual improvement, hence change, through time—is indeed a myth."[2]

The point made by Professor Eldredge is very clearly illustrated by the fossil data relating to the extinct hominid species *Homo erectus*. The well-documented fossil record of this important hominid spans a period of over a million years, from his initial appearance until his extinction (see Appendix B). What significant evolutionary changes do the fossil data show for *Homo erectus* over such a long period of time? The answer is: *none at all*.

Professor Steven M. Stanley of Johns Hopkins University writes of *Homo erectus:* "This species existed with little change for more than a million years."[3] Professor David Pilbeam of Harvard University writes: "In that span of time, well over a million years, the physical record of *Homo erectus* is one of prolonged morphological stability."[4] In other words, *Homo erectus* did not undergo *any* significant evolutionary changes throughout the million years of his existence.

We next consider the "evolutionary history" of the most recent hominid species—Modern Man. The fossil data show that Modern Man appeared *suddenly* only 40,000 years ago. "We have the appearance, apparently pretty abruptly everywhere, of men of completely modern aspect."[5] Since his sudden appearance, Modern Man has persisted without change to the present day. The hominid species that preceded Modern Man, and is most similar to him, is Neanderthal Man, who appeared approximately 100,000 years ago. Neanderthal Man existed without change for about 60,000 years.[6] Then, for unknown reasons, all Neanderthal Men *suddenly* disappeared. "The departure can only be called abrupt."[7] All these data are inconsistent with the idea of gradual evolution.

Our final question involves the relationship between Modern Man and Neanderthal Man. Did Modern Men evolve from the Neanderthal Men that preceded them? Professor Eldredge is convinced by the fossil evidence that "the Neanderthals cannot have borne any direct ancestral relationship to ourselves."[8] Professor Stanley writes regarding Modern Man: "Out of nowhere, our sharp chin, weak brow, and high vaulted forehead appear in the fossil record. These particular features are utterly unpredictable on the basis of what preceded them."[9] *The Cambridge Encyclopedia of Archaeology* concludes that "there is no evidence to indicate the local evolution of Neanderthals into anatomically modern people."[10]

THE PALEOLITHIC AGE

The first appearance of stone tools about two million years ago marks the beginning of what archaeologists call the Paleolithic Age ("Old Stone Age"). It is important to realize that even the most advanced paleolithic stone tools look *extremely* primitive when compared to any contemporary tool. Indeed, a typical paleolithic tool consists merely of a piece of flint that has been sharpened by hammering off a few flakes, or the sharp flakes themselves may be the tools. The process of paleolithic toolmaking is so simple that "in only a few hours, most novices can master the basic mechanics of stone flaking."[11] The resulting tools are equally simple. In fact, if a layman were to find such a tool, it is doubtful that he would even recognize it as man-made. To the untrained eye, a paleolithic tool looks quite similar to the sharp stones that are commonly found lying around. Any illustration of paleolithic tools will confirm this.[12]

Another point that should be stressed is that the use of simple tools is by no means a uniquely human activity. "We know today that toolmaking and use, in the strictest sense, are not our own exclusive province. . . . Chimpanzees strip and prepare twigs to 'fish' for termites in their earthen mounds. Capuchin monkeys use stones to crack open hard nuts. Baboons kill scorpions with rocks before removing their stingers and eating them."[13] It has been observed that "some chimpanzees make tools for future use. . . . What is more, the behavior is learned: young chimpanzees become proficient by imitating their elders."[14]

The quotations given above are *not* intended to imply that the early hominids were technologically no more advanced than monkeys. On the other hand, one must keep in mind that the making and using of simple tools does *not* qualify a hominid to be characterized as "almost human." Professor David Pilbeam of Harvard University has emphasized just this point: "The early hominds were, after all, markedly different from any [human being] living today. In many instances, however, these differences have been ignored and early hominids have been made to seem too much like modern human beings."[15]

NEANDERTHAL MAN

It is not "fair" to compare the enormous technological achievements of contemporary Modern Man with the simple tools made by paleolithic hominids. Our large brains give us such an obvious advantage. However, there is one exception to the pattern of earlier hominids having smaller brains. That exception is Neanderthal Man (see Appendix B). "The brain encased in the Neanderthal skull was on the average slightly larger than the brain of Modern Man."[16]

How advanced was the toolmaking technology developed by Neanderthal Man? "Most of the Neanderthals' tools were flakes of flint, struck from a 'core' and trimmed into projectile points, knives and scrapers."[17]

By comparison, let us consider some of the tools developed by Modern Man, who has thus far existed for a shorter time than Neanderthal Man. The "tools" of Modern Man include the computer, the laser, the transistor, and the space satellite, to say nothing of jet planes and nuclear-powered submarines. This brief list is quite sufficient to show that any comparison between the technological developments of Neanderthal Man and those of Modern Man is absolutely ludicrous.

What about the arts? In this area, the best that can be said for Neanderthal Man is that "fragments of mineral colouring matter, ground smooth or shaped into pointed pencils, have been found in many sites, although it is not known what surfaces they may have been intended to decorate."[18] In other words, fragments of paints have been found, but no art work of any sort exists that can be attributed to Neanderthal Man.

By comparison, we note the rich tradition of Modern Man in painting, sculpture, music, architecture, and many other art forms. Once again, one finds a striking contrast between the enormous artistic achievements of Modern Man and the complete lack of art that characterizes Neanderthal Man.

It is important to mention that the magnificent cave paintings found in southwestern France and elsewhere were *all* the work of Modern Man.[19] No cave was ever decorated by Neanderthal Man.[20]

Didn't the Neanderthals do anything not directly connected with keeping alive? Yes, they buried their dead.[21] However, this single sign of Neanderthal "culture" is utterly insignificant when compared to the vast cultural achievements of Modern Man in all branches of knowledge—science, philosophy, medicine, literature, art, mathematics, music, etc.

How can one explain the enormous disparity between the accomplishments of Modern Man and those of Neanderthal Man? The fact is that scientists have no explanation. What *is* clear is that these vast intellectual and cultural differences are *not* due to physical differences between the two species. Neanderthal Man did not suffer from any physical shortcomings relative to Modern Man. A comparison between the anatomy and size of the Neanderthal brain and the modern brain "does not suggest any differences in intellectual or behavioral capacities."[22] Anatomically speaking, "Neanderthals were not less human than modern men. . . . It is now clear that the Neanderthals had the same postural abilities, manual dexterity, and range and character of movement that modern men do . . . [they had] a much stronger grip than that of modern men, but there was nothing gorilla-like in it; their control of movement was evidently the same as ours."[23]

MODERN MAN

Modern Man first appeared about 40,000 years ago, and he *immediately* showed his *marked* cultural superiority relative to

95

Neanderthal Man. The archaeological data are so striking that every scientific account emphasizes the dramatic, far-reaching cultural advances rapidly introduced by Modern Man. A few quotations will illustrate the point.

> The toolmaking industries of Modern Man are completely different from those of Neanderthal Man. . . . this new tool kit reflects a quantum leap in hunting techniques—and, by extension, in mental abilities. . . . The Modern Men who succeeded the Neanderthals were not only vastly better hunters, but were their intellectual superiors in every way.[24]

> Then came the great acceleration of about 40,000 years ago. . . . Its fruits included entirely new and complex tools and weapons, the construction of shelters, the invention of boats, the addition of fish to the human diet, deep-water voyages (to Australia, for example), the peopling of the Arctic, the migration to the Americas and the proliferation of a lively variety of arts and a wide range of personal adornment.[25]

> In Europe 35,000 years ago, where the archaeological record is by far the clearest, what we see is an abrupt transition. . . . the cultural kit bag, the stone implements, changes radically and suddenly. No gradual transitions here. Cave art appears, also with no premonitory signs.[26]

> Important behavioral changes are evident in the archaeological record. They include a proliferation of superior stone and bone tools, shifts in hunting patterns, in the use and control of fire, in the use of clothing, in settlement patterns, in population size, in ecological range, in art and other evidences of ritual activity. All of this points to the emergence of a species possessing modern behavioral capabilities and potential.[27]

> It is interesting that between 40,000 and 35,000 years ago, there was a marked increase in complexity of the sociocultural system of the hominids. Soon thereafter, various forms of art are a regular feature at archaeological sites [with] a rapid increase in its complexity. . . . The Upper Paleolithic [Modern Man] introduces art: cave paintings, engravings on bone, statuettes of bone and stone, and such personal decoration as strings of beads. The Middle Paleolithic [Neanderthal Man] is devoid of such expressions.[28]

It should be emphasized once again that there are *no* physical differences between Modern Man and Neanderthal Man that would lead one to expect such sudden and dramatic cultural changes. The average brain size is the same for the two species,[29] and in all physical characteristics and manual skills, Neanderthal Man was the equal of Modern Man.[30] Nevertheless, the enormous cultural and intellectual superiority of Modern Man over Neanderthal Man is unmistakenly recorded in the archaeological record.

THE AGRICULTURAL REVOLUTION

After the initial explosion of cultural progress that marked his appearance, Modern Man continued his technological and artistic development, but at a much slower pace. Then, about 10,000 years ago, another explosion of cultural progress occurred, of even greater dimensions than previously. In fact, this was the most comprehensive series of cultural advances that has ever taken place, covering all aspects of human behavior. The cumulative effect of all these changes was literally to revolutionize society. These many fundamental advances are collectively called the Agricultural Revolution or the Neolithic Revolution. This revolution was so all-encompassing that archaeologists consider it to be *the* major milestone in prehistoric chronology. (As indicated in Appendix B, earlier times are denoted as the Paleolithic Age [Old Stone Age], whereas subsequent times are denoted as the Neolithic Age [New Stone Age].)

The fundamental cultural innovations that occurred at or shortly after the Agricultural Revolution include the following:

1. the origin of agriculture
2. the origin of animal husbandry
3. the development of metalworking
4. the invention of the wheel
5. the first written language
6. the development of ceramic pottery
7. the origin of weaving
8. the making of bread, wine, and dairy products (cheese and butter)
9. the development of musical instruments
10. advanced architecture

All these cultural advances—and others—resulted in the complex social organization that soon gave rise to the first cities and thus to civilization (whose literal meaning is "city making") as we know it today. The enormous range of these rapid and profound cultural developments is emphasized in every archaeological account of this period. A few quotations (which will also serve as references for the preceding list of cultural innovations) will illustrate the point.

Thus, in 3000 or 4000 years, the life of man had changed more radically than in all the preceding 250,000 years. Before the Agricultural Revolution, most men must have spent their waking moments seeking their next meal. . . . As man learned to produce food and store it in the grain bin and on the hoof, he was able to settle in larger communities. . . . Such innovations as the discovery of the basic mechanical principles, weaving, the plow, the wheel and metallurgy soon appeared.[31]

One cannot avoid being impressed at how rapidly the transition from Paleolithic hunting to regionally organized communities occurred. . . . the domestication of plants and animals and the establishment of settled farming communities . . . the development of pottery . . . painted and decorated pots developed quite rapidly. . . . Bronze tools and weapons were produced. Writing evolved from pictographic notations, while specialized artisans made quantities of diverse goods. . . . market centers became towns. . . . The urban revolution was under way, the world of people was being transformed and the first civilizations were taking shape.[32]

The development of plant and animal domestication has often been called the Neolithic Revolution. . . . Once set in motion, the changes arising from food production so altered human social life that all manner of new developments came into being . . . village ways of life, population growth . . . and increasingly complex forms of social organization.[33]

The results of the domestication [of animals] were certainly revolutionary—being, along with the cultivation of plants, the essential first step toward civilization.[34]

The achievement of our species was the Agricultural Revolution. . . . With the domestication of plants and animals, vast new dimensions for cultural evolution suddenly became possible.[35]

Major characteristics of agricultural economies began to be evident. . . . animal domestication and more advanced cultivation techniques, like irrigation, were integrated into agricultural systems. . . . This process occurred with explosive consequences . . . the pace of change in key areas was so rapid and their effects so far-reaching.[36]

Starting about 10,000 years ago, agriculture was invented and spread . . . populations increased enormously in density.[37]

Agriculture and animal husbandry appeared at roughly the same time around the globe. Technological progress, the mastery of new materials (such as metals) and new energy sources (such as wind and water power). . . . The acceleration of human history cannot be better illustrated than by comparing the changes of the past 10,000 years with those of the previous four million years.[38]

What was the cause of the Agricultural Revolution? What triggered all these "explosive" and "radical," indeed "revolutionary" changes that so altered human society? The answer is that no one really knows.[39]

Why, after many hundreds of millenniums of subsistence by hunting and gathering, did man only quite recently adopt the alternate strategy of cultivating crops and husbanding animals? The reasons for this dramatic shift remain a topic of debate.[40]

It is tempting to suppose that some disruption of established ways provided the challenge and stimulus to undertake deliberate cultivation and new tools. What exactly these events were, and what the stimulus was, we do not know.[41]

THE BIBLICAL TEXT

Having described the recent archaeological findings and the fossil evidence relating to man, we are in a position to make a comparison between the biblical text and current scientific knowledge. We shall relate to the questions that were raised at the beginning of this chapter.

1. The archaeological record shows that the appearance of contemporary Modern Man was accompanied by a series of unprecedented advances in human culture. Moreover, these

changes occurred *suddenly*—archaeologists speak of "an abrupt transition"[42] in the cultural level, marked by "radical changes." In addition to the suddenness of these events ("with no premonitory signs"[43]), scientific accounts of the archaeological data invariably comment, often in great surprise, on the vast scope of the changes introduced by Modern Man. These innovations extend to every aspect of human endeavor, ranging from "a proliferation of superior tools"[44] to "the proliferation of a variety of arts"[45] to a long and impressive list of "entirely new"[46] technologies and inventions. The cultural superiority of Modern Man is so remarkable that the scientific literature characterizes contemporary human beings as "intellectual superiors in every way"[47] over all previous hominids, displaying "a quantum leap in mental abilities"[48] which "points to the emergence of a species possessing modern behavioral capabilities and potential."[49]

In view of this archaeological evidence, the biblical statement that man was created "in the image of God" (1:27) may be understood as referring to the unique mental gifts bestowed upon Modern Man. These gifts have enabled him to produce the enormous range of cultural changes that appeared so suddenly and dramatically in the archaeological record. Indeed, the uniqueness of Modern Man is quite obvious from the archaeological data.

Modern Man's cultural progress continues unabated to the present day. Of all hominid species, *only* Modern Man explores the galaxies of outer space and probes the inner structure of the atom. Man has developed instant worldwide communications and has built electronic computers that can perform millions of operations each second. Man literally stands on the moon, transplants human hearts, and through genetic engineering, constructs new living organisms. Man excels in the arts, the sciences, and all other branches of knowledge. All these—and more—are the achievements that characterize Modern Man.

It is particularly meaningful that Modern Man is intellectually and culturally so *vastly superior* to his closest relative, the extinct Neanderthal Man, even though both species are *physically very similar*. They possess the same average brain size[50] as well as "the same postural abilities, manual dexterity and range of movement."[51] Scientists have no explanation for the enormous difference in intellectual attainments between Modern Man and Neanderthal Man. They are puzzled by the fact that a comparison between the physical features of these two species "does not suggest any differences in intellectual or behavioral capacities."[52] In contrast to the secular scientist, one who believes in God *does* have an explanation for the uniqueness of Modern Man—an explanation that is written in verse 1:27: "And God created man in His image."

As previously noted with reference to the creation of the animals, the biblical expression "God created man" does *not* imply creation in the physical sense (something out of nothing).[53] Almost all traditional Jewish biblical commentators explain that the verb "create" regarding man refers to the creation of the unique intellectual and spiritual capabilities that characterize human beings. In their discussions of Genesis 2:7, Rashi, Saadiah Gaon, Sforno, Radak, and Ramban all comment that man's superiority over the other species lies in the areas of knowledge, speech, and intellect. Indeed, *physically*, Modern Man is a very ordinary creature, quite similar to many other primate species.

We also note that the word "man" (Hebrew *Adam*) in the biblical phrase "And God created man" is to be understood as a generic term denoting the contemporary human species as a whole rather than a particular person (i.e., Adam). Sforno points out, in his discussion of Genesis 1:26, that throughout the sixth day of creation, the word "man" always "refers to the species of living creatures known as man." Sforno further comments that the use of the word "man" to indicate mankind in general occurs again in verse 2:7.

2. The appearance of Modern Man was marked by a dramatic surge of cultural advances. This was followed by a long period of gradual technological and artistic development. Then there occurred another sudden, even more dramatic and far-reaching surge of cultural innovation that covered all aspects of human activity. This latter cultural explosion, which took place only a few thousand years ago, has been designated by archaeologists as the Agricultural Revolution or the Neolithic Revolution.

This relatively recent "revolution" can be associated with the biblical statement that God blessed man, telling him to "fill the land and subdue it" (1:28). Scientific accounts of the Agricultural Revolution elaborate on the vast and sudden changes that took place in every phase of human society ("the life of man was changed radically"[54] as man subdued the land, and "populations increased enormously"[55] as man filled the land). This remarkable revolution was characterized by the cultivation of food plants and by the domestication of animals, which "occurred with explosive consequences."[56] The all-encompassing nature of the divine blessing bestowed upon man is very clear from the description of events reported by archaeologists.

The scientific evidence indicates that "In 3000 or 4000 years, the life of man changed more radically than in all the preceding 250,000 years before the Agricultural Revolution."[57] Thus, the fulfillment of the divine will is recorded in the archaeological data.

NOTES

1. N. Eldredge and I. Tattersall, *The Myths of Human Evolution* (New York: Columbia University Press, 1982), p. 120.

2. Ibid., p. 2.

3. S. M. Stanley, *The New Evolutionary Timetable* (New York: Basic Books, 1981), p. 147.

4. D. Pilbeam, *Scientific American*, vol. 250, March 1984, p. 68.

5. Eldredge and Tattersall, p. 155.

6. E. Trinkhaus and W. W. Howells, *Scientific American*, vol. 241, December 1979, pp. 94–105. This article, entitled "The Neanderthals," contains an excellent account of current knowledge concerning Neanderthal Man.

7. Ibid., p. 101.

8. Eldredge and Tattersall, p. 155.

9. Stanley, p. 151.

10. A. Sherratt, ed., *The Cambridge Encyclopedia of Archaeology* (Cambridge: At the University Press, 1980), p. 88.

11. N. Toth, *Scientific American*, vol. 256, April 1987, p. 109.

12. A series of Oldowan-style tools and Acheulean-style tools (these terms denote different paleolithic toolmaking cultures) are illustrated in ibid., p. 108.

13. Eldredge and Tattersall, pp. 8–9.

14. Toth, pp. 104, 111.

15. Pilbeam, p. 60.

16. Trinkhaus and Howells, p. 97.

17. Ibid., p. 94.

18. Sherratt, p. 85.

19. A. Leroi-Gourhan, *Scientific American*, vol. 246, June 1982, pp. 80–88.

20. Trinkhaus and Howells, p. 94.

21. Sherratt, p. 85.

22. Trinkhaus and Howells, p. 97.

23. Ibid., p. 99.

24. Eldredge and Tattersall, pp. 154, 159.

25. S. L. Washburn, *Scientific American*, vol. 239, September 1978, p. 154.

26. N. Eldredge, *Time Frames* (New York: Simon & Schuster, 1985), p. 87.

27. Pilbeam, p. 69.

28. Trinkhaus and Howells, pp. 94, 105.

29. Ibid., p. 97.

30. Ibid., p. 99.

31. R. J. Braidwood, *Scientific American*, vol. 203, September 1960, p. 148.

32. E. A. Hoebel and T. Weaver, *Anthropology and the Human Experience* (New York: McGraw-Hill, 1979), pp. 183, 195, 201.

33. G. H. Pelto and P. J. Pelto, *The Cultural Dimensions of the Human Adventure* (New York: Macmillan, 1979), p. 93.

34. M. L. Ryder, *Sheep and Man* (London: Gerald Duckworth, 1983), p. 17.

35. Braidwood, p. 131.

36. A. Sherratt, p. 407.

37. E. O. Wilson, *Sociobiology: The New Synthesis* (Cambridge, Mass.: Harvard University Press, 1975), p. 569.

38. Washburn, p. 154.

39. Climatic changes are sometimes suggested as the triggering mechanism because the Ice Age ended about 10,000 years ago. However, other workers point out that this suggestion would be more appropriate to Central and Northern Europe than to the warm climate of the Middle East, where the Agricultural Revolution began.

40. L. G. Straus et al., *Scientific American*, vol. 242, June 1980, p. 128.

41. H. H. Lamb, *Climate, History and the Modern World* (London: Methuen, 1982), p. 122.

42. Eldredge, p. 87.

43. Ibid.,

44. Pilbeam, p. 69.

45. Washburn, p. 154.

46. Ibid.

47. Eldredge and Tattersall, p. 159.

48. Ibid., p. 154.

49. Pilbeam. p. 69.

50. Trinkhaus and Howells, p. 97.

51. Ibid., p. 99.

52. Ibid., p. 97.

53. This point is discussed in the chapter dealing with the fifth day of creation (pt. II).

54. Braidwood, p. 148.

55. Wilson, p. 569.

56. Sherratt, p. 407.

57. Braidwood, p. 148.

The Sixth Day (Part II)
Man as the Pinnacle
of Creation

GENESIS—CHAPTER I

²⁷*And God created man in His image; in the image of God, He created him; male and female He created them.* ²⁸*And God blessed them and God said to them, "Be fruitful and multiply, and fill the land and subdue it; and rule over the fish of the sea, and over the winged creatures of the air, and over every living creature that crawls upon the earth." ²⁹And God said, "Behold, I have given you every herb yielding seed which is on all the land, and every tree which has fruit bearing seed; for you it shall be for food."*

QUESTIONS

At the conclusion of the six days of creation, Genesis 1:27–29 strongly implies that the entire universe exists solely for the benefit of man. To be convinced of the absurdity of such a claim, one need only consider the distant stars. The universe is filled with many billions of stars. What possible relevance to man could there be in all the countless stars that stretch across the vast expanses of outer space? In fact, before the recent invention of powerful telescopes, no one was even aware that so many stars existed. The belief that there is some connection between man and the distant stars is mere astrology and superstition.

The foregoing represents the popular view. We shall now present the scientific evidence that provides an explanation of the biblical text.

THE DISTANT STARS

Recent advances in astronomy have revealed a remarkable link between life on earth and the distant stars. In fact, it is no exaggeration to say that without the stars, life on earth would have been impossible.

The bodies of all living organisms contain the chemical elements carbon, hydrogen, oxygen, and nitrogen, plus smaller but crucial amounts of several other elements. What is the origin of these chemical elements?

According to the firmly established modern theory of cosmology,[1] a few moments after the beginning of the universe, the only chemical elements that existed were hydrogen and helium. There was neither carbon nor oxygen nor nitrogen nor any other element essential for life. These elements were formed only much later, in the blazing interior of large stars. Professor Michael Zeilik of the University of New Mexico explains:

The massive stars have lifetimes of only a few millions to tens of millions of years, after which they catastrophically explode. During their short life span, the thermonuclear furnace deep within them manufactures elements as heavy as carbon and iron; at their death, the awesome violence of the supernova explosion forges elements heavier than iron and blasts as much as 90% of the star's material into interstellar space. Out of this recycled material, new stars and planets will be born: stars such as the Sun and planets such as the Earth. Moreover, life arose on our planet because massive stars lived and died; without supernova explosions, the carbon that is the key to life as we know it would not be distributed throughout interstellar space.[2]

These results were discovered recently. *The Cambridge Encyclopedia of Astronomy* writes:

It used to be supposed that the universe has always had the composition we observe today. . . . It is not, perhaps, widely appreciated that all the atoms on Earth [except hydrogen] had to be created inside a generation of stars that evolved before the birth of the Sun and planets. The elucidation of this process by which elements were and are created in the cosmic environment will stand in history as one of the greatest advances of the physical sciences in the twentieth century.[3]

The same encyclopedia describes the essential relationship between life on earth and the formation of the elements in the interior of the distant stars:

All common materials of our world were made in stellar furnaces before our Sun and planets formed; every atom of our bodies was fused together in past aeons of an almost fantastic galactic history. In truth, we are the children of the Universe.[4]

There is yet another important connection between ourselves and the stars, which relates to the vast distances that separate us from them. It is now recognized that these distances are crucial to our existence. Stellar explosions emit not only the chemical elements that are essential for life; they also emit "cosmic radiation," which is deadly. We are saved from cosmic radiation *only* because the stars are so very far away from our planet. Over the enormous distances that cosmic radiation must travel before reaching the earth, it becomes so reduced in intensity that it is no longer harmful. Professor Freeman J. Dyson of the Institute for Advanced Study in Princeton explains:

> The vastness of the interstellar spaces has diluted the cosmic rays enough to save us from being fried or at least sterilized by them. If sheer distance had not effectively isolated the quiet regions of the universe from the noisy ones, no type of biological [system] would have been possible.[5]

THE BIBLICAL TEXT

Having described some recent findings in astronomy that relate to man, we are in a position to make a comparison between the biblical text and current scientific knowledge. We shall relate to the question that was raised at the beginning of this chapter.

It is a fundamental principle of the sages of the Talmud that man is the pinnacle of creation, and that everything in the universe was formed for his benefit.[6] Nowhere is this principle demonstrated more strikingly than in the recent scientific discovery that even the distant stars played a vital role in making it possible for man to exist. ("Life arose on our planet because massive stars lived and died."[7]) It is now recognized that all the chemical elements that are necessary for life (except hydrogen) were originally formed deep in the interior of the stars. These elements were later ejected into space when a star underwent a violent supernova explosion. Eventually, the chemicals reached our solar system to form the living tissues of plants, animals, and man. ("In truth, we are the children of the Universe."[8])

The explosion of distant stars is merely one example of a large number of different events that were necessary for the existence and well-being of man. Indeed, the numerous "accidents of nature" that seem to have happened for our benefit are so remarkable that many scientists have commented on this phenomenon. Particularly perceptive are the impressions of Professor Freeman J. Dyson of the Institute for Advanced Study in Princeton:

> As we look out into the universe and identify the many accidents of physics and astronomy that have worked together to our benefit, it almost seems as if the universe must in some sense have known that we were coming.[9]

We note the harmony between these words of a world-famous secular scientist and the writings of the talmudic sages.[10]

MAN IN THE IMAGE OF GOD

In the previous chapter, we pointed out that the biblical description of man as being "in the image of God" (1:27) refers to the unique intellectual and creative faculties with which man has been endowed by his Creator. We conclude with a discussion of three aspects of man's uniqueness.

Communication

The past few thousand years have witnessed the enormous progress made by man in all areas of intellectual endeavor. An essential ingredient of this progress is the unique ability of members of the human species to communicate with each other. This enables man to benefit from the accomplishments of his predecessors. The distinguished physicist Isaac Newton once remarked: "If I have seen further [than others], it is by standing upon the shoulders of Giants."

The importance of communication can hardly be overestimated. Indeed, many biblical commentators characterize the uniqueness of man in terms of his ability to speak. Onkelos, the second-century translator of the Bible into Aramaic, designates man as "the speaking being" in his rendering of Genesis 2:7. Similarly, in their comments on the same verse, Rashi, Saadiah Gaon, Sforno, and Ramban all state that man's superiority over the animals lies in his powers of speech and reason.

The technological innovations that have revolutionized human society were the result of the cumulative efforts of many talented people. Because man can communicate, a scientist need not "reinvent the wheel" before making new contributions. The fact that one can build upon the work of others has led to the rapid technological progress that is the hallmark of civilization.

Man's ability to communicate with his fellows is one aspect of man's being created "in the image of God."

Intellectual Curiosity

Man is the only species that displays intellectual curiosity regarding matters that do not directly enhance his chances for survival. All other species concern themselves exclusively with food, shelter, safety, mating, etc., for themselves and for their family, tribe, or colony. By contrast, human beings express great interest in and devote time to the pursuit of knowledge and art which have no practical consequences.

There is no clearer illustration of this phenomenon than the book that you presently hold in your hand. Reading this book will *not* increase your salary, will *not* put better food on your table, and will *not* in any way improve your physical situation. Nevertheless, in spite of the complete absence of any tangible benefit, you persist in reading in order to satisfy your intellectual curiosity.

Man's intellectual curiosity is another aspect of his being created "in the image of God."

Conscience

The most striking feature of man's uniqueness lies in the realm of conscience and morality. Man, and *only* man, is capable of making decisions based on the abstract principles of right and wrong. A man may sacrifice his personal welfare, and indeed even his life, in the cause of morality.

The current plight of millions of starving people in North Africa has generated a worldwide appeal for help. These Africans have nothing at all in common with the average American or European—neither race nor religion nor language nor ideology nor life-style. Yet the sight of starving children on the TV screen touches the viewer's heart, and his conscience "demands" of him that he contribute to help alleviate the suffering.

Of all the species in the animal kingdom, only man deals with moral problems. And only man possesses the spiritual faculties for making moral judgments. This divine privilege and accompanying responsibility are ours alone, because only man was created "in the image of God."

"Behold, I have set before you this day life and good, and death and evil . . . therefore choose life" (Deuteronomy 30:15, 19).

NOTES

1. A detailed description of the big-bang theory of cosmology is give in the chapter dealing with the first day of creation.

2. M. Zeilik, *Scientific American*, vol. 238, April 1978, p. 110.

3. S. Mitton, ed.-in-chief, *The Cambridge Encyclopedia of Astronomy* (London: Jonathan Cape, 1977), pp. 121, 123.

4. Ibid., p. 125.

5. F. J. Dyson, *Scientific American*, vol. 225, September 1971, p. 57.

6. For example, "Adam was created on the eve of the Sabbath, and why? In order that he [Adam] should enter upon his meal immediately. A parable: For this can be compared to a king of flesh and blood who built a palace and perfected it and prepared a meal, and after that brought in the guests" (Babylonian Talmud, Sanhedrin 38a).

7. Zeilik, p. 110.

8. Mitton, p. 125.

9. Dyson, p. 59.

10. See above, n. 6.

After the Six Days
The Early History
of Man

¹*And Adam knew Eve his wife; and she conceived and bore Cain, saying, "I have gotten a man from the Lord."* ²*And again she bore his brother Abel. And Abel was a shepherd, and Cain was a tiller of the ground.*

¹⁹*And Lamech took for himself two wives; the name of one was Adah, and the name of the other was Zillah.* ²⁰*And Adah bore Jabal; he was the father of those who dwell in tents and have cattle.* ²¹*And his brother's name was Jubal; he was the father of all those who handle the harp and flute.* ²²*And Zillah, she also bore Tubal-cain, who sharpened every instrument of copper and iron; and the sister of Tubal-cain was Naamah.*

The period after the six days of creation is, strictly speaking, beyond the scope of this book. Nevertheless, it is worthwhile to include some subjects from a subsequent chapter of the Book of Genesis in order to demonstrate that agreement between current scientific knowledge and the biblical text is not limited to the six days of creation.

QUESTIONS

After concluding the six days of creation, the Book of Genesis continues with an account of the early history of man. The archaeological events that are described in the fourth chapter of Genesis are extremely problematic.

We read that the sons of Adam engaged in agriculture and animal husbandry (4:2), strongly implying that these two activities were initiated simultaneously at about that time. We subsequently read that the sons of Lamech originated the craft of metalworking and the making of musical instruments (4:21-22). It is well known that such major technological and cultural advances evolved only very gradually, in the course of many tens of thousands of years. The claim that these complex changes in human society occurred *suddenly*, only a few thousand years ago, is completely contradicted by extensive archaeological evidence.

The above represents the popular view. We shall now present the scientific evidence that provides an explanation of the biblical text that is consistent with current scientific knowledge.

AGRICULTURE AND ANIMAL HUSBANDRY

In a previous chapter, we described in detail the "cultural explosion" of ten thousand years ago that archaeologists have named the Agricultural Revolution.[1] As the name implies, the characteristic feature of this revolution was the origin of agriculture. However, a curious aspect of the Agricultural Revolution was that the beginning of agriculture was closely linked to the beginning of animal husbandry.[2]

Archaeological evidence and pollen analysis . . . from Turkey, Syria, Iraq and Iran indicate that about the same time, man was beginning to domesticate animals and food grains."[3]

Along with the planting of wild grain, there are ample signs of the domestication of wild goats and sheep, as well as of asses and dogs. Thus, the first farming may well have been mixed farming.[4]

The close association between agriculture and animal husbandry was unexpected. "Several prominent scholars have wondered whether the cultivation of cereals and the breeding of animals, which appeared together from the beginning [of the Agricultural Revolution], was coincidental or due to fundamental causes."[5]

Although the *cause* remains a subject of debate, the *facts* are clear—the beginning of agriculture and the beginning of animal husbandry appear *simultaneously* in the archaeological record; these events mark the onset of the Agricultural Revolution.

METALWORKING AND MUSICAL INSTRUMENTS

The earliest archaeological records of metalworking date from the period known as the Chalcolithic Age, which occurred after the Agricultural Revolution.[6] At that time, metalworking consisted of forging and shaping native metals—primarily copper.

The earliest archaeological evidence for stringed musical instruments is the imprint of a lute that appears on two clay cylinder seals dating from the Akkadian dynasty in Mesopotamia, nearly 5000 years ago.[7]

Although wind instruments are ancient, the early flutes were very primitive, and consisted only of a hollow tube. Eventually, flutes were fashioned with finger holes, which permitted the playing of several different notes. Such nonprimitive flutes first appeared after the Agricultural Revolution.[8]

In summary, the craft of metalworking, the invention of stringed instruments, and the development of nonprimitive wind instruments *all* date from about the same time, namely, *after* the beginning of the Agricultural Revolution.

THE BIBLICAL TEXT

Having described some recent findings in archaeology, we are in a position to make a comparison between the biblical text and current scientific knowledge.

The Agricultural Revolution was characterized by the first cultivation of food plants, and simultaneously, the domestication of animals. ("Agriculture and animal husbandry appeared at roughly the same time."[9]) One of the most striking features of this revolution was the great rapidity with which these fundamental cultural changes took place. ("One cannot avoid being impressed by how rapidly the transition occurred."[10]) These events can be associated with the biblical statement (Genesis 4:2) that the family of Adam engaged in both agriculture and animal husbandry ("And Abel was a shepherd, and Cain was a tiller of the ground").

The Agricultural Revolution was followed by an enormous number of important technological innovations that appeared in rapid succession. These innovations include the craft of metalworking, and the making of musical instruments, such as stringed instruments and wind instruments. These inventions and techniques, which were developed almost simultaneously, can be associated with the biblical statement (Genesis 4:21–22) that the family of Lamech initiated the use of stringed and wind musical instruments ("Jubal . . . was the father of all those who handle the harp and flute") and originated the craft of metalworking ("she also bore Tubal-cain, who sharpened every instrument of copper and iron").

NOTES

1. R. J. Braidwood, *Scientific American*, vol. 203, September 1960, pp. 130–148.
2. B. Gunda, *Tools and Tillage*, vol. 5, 1986, p. 156.
3. H. H. Lamb, *Climate, History and the Modern World* (London: Methuen, 1982), p. 112.
4. R. Pearson, *Anthropology* (New York: Holt, Rinehart & Winston, 1974), p. 348.
5. J. Troels-Smith, *Tools and Tillage*, vol. 5, 1984, p. 14.
6. S. L. Semiatin and G. D. Lahoti, *Scientific American*, vol. 245, August 1981, p. 82. A. Sherratt, ed. *The Cambridge Encyclopedia of Archaeology* (Cambridge: At the University Press, 1980), p. 11. J. Dayton, *Minerals, Metals, Glazing and Man* (London: George Harrap, 1978), p. 136. N. H. Gale and Z. Stos-Gale, *Scientific American*, vol. 244, June 1981, p. 142.
7. D. Collon and A. D. Kilmer, in *Music and Civilization*, edited by T. C. Mitchell (London: British Museum Publications, 1980), p. 13.
8. K. Geiringer, *Instruments in the History of Western Music* (London: George Allen & Unwin, 1978), pp. 29–30.
9. S. L. Washburn, *Scientific American*, vol. 239, September 1978, p. 154.
10. E. A. Hoebel and T. Weaver, *Anthropology and the Human Experience* (New York: McGraw-Hill, 1979), p. 195.

REFLECTIONS

In this concluding chapter, we discuss a number of topics that relate to our analysis of the first chapter of the Book of Genesis.

SCIENCE AND THE BOOK OF GENESIS

The goal of this book has been to show that there is consistency between contemporary scientific knowledge and the literal meaning of the first chapter of the Book of Genesis. The analysis presented here has demonstrated that many biblical passages can indeed be understood in terms of present-day science. Nevertheless, we certainly do not pretend that everything has been explained. Rather, we view this work as but one step towards revealing the harmony that exists between the biblical text and the science of the twentieth century. Although much remains to be done, the results of this step are encouraging.

Throughout the discussion, we have been careful to base our analysis on scientific ideas that are firmly established and buttressed by extensive evidence. Nevertheless, it is inevitable that some parts of the analysis will require revision as additional scientific data become available. However, we expect the basic pattern to remain intact. In fact, we anticipate that the scientific knowledge of the future will lead to additional understanding and new insights into those biblical passages that are still unclear.

BIBLICAL CHRONOLOGY

As discussed in the introduction, the view adopted in this book is that six days of creation are *not* six periods of twenty-four hours each. Rather, they are six phases in the development of the universe—from the initial creation to the appearance of man. Moreover, we have shown that this approach is consistent with the view of many traditional biblical commentators. Nevertheless, the question still remains: Why does the term "day" appear throughout the first chapter of the Book of Genesis if a twenty-four-hour period of time is not intended?

The use of the word "day" in the first chapter can be understood in terms of the first three verses of the second chapter, which discuss the seventh day—the Sabbath. This day was designated as holy because it marked the completion of the creation of the universe.[1] The connection between the Sabbath and the creation is reinforced by the discussion of the seventh day that appears in the Ten Commandments. We read that the reason that God sanctified the Sabbath was to have this day serve as a weekly reminder of the fact that God created the universe (Exodus 20:8–11). However, the Sabbath *is* an actual day of twenty-four hours. Therefore, the six phases of creation were *also* referred to as "days" in order to strengthen the connection between the Sabbath and the creation of the universe.

THE "SIX DAYS"

The six phases of the development of the universe—the "six days"—fall into two cycles. The first cycle, comprising four phases, deals with the formation of the infrastructure of the universe that is necessary for the existence and well-being of man. The second cycle, comprising two phases, deals with the formation of the animal kingdom, which culminates in the appearance of man.

The building of the infrastructure of the universe is divided by the Book of Genesis into the following four phases:

First day: creation of the universe
Second day: formation of the solar system
Third day: formation of the continents and oceans on earth; appearance of green plants
Fourth day: fixing the present-day seasons

It should be mentioned that the biblical order of these four phases corresponds to the actual sequence in which these events occurred.

The formation of the animal kingdom, leading up to man, is divided by the Book of Genesis into the following two phases:

Fifth day: marine and winged animals
Sixth day: mammals and other terrestrial animals; man

It is interesting to note that the biblical text places the formation of the plants on a completely different footing from the formation of the animals. From the biological point of view, there is of course no essential difference between plants and animals. But Genesis is not a biology textbook. In its view, the plants are objects whose function is to serve man by providing him with food, clothing (linen, cotton), shelter (wood), etc. Therefore, the plants are associated with the first cycle of four phases that deal with the infrastructure of the universe. By contrast, Genesis describes the animals as sharing with man the characteristic features of living creatures. Therefore, the animals are associated with the second cycle of two phases that deal with man.

CREATION

The phrase "God created" occurs three times in the first chapter of Genesis. These phrases refer to the three different acts of creation that are described in the biblical text: (1) the creation of the universe, (2) the creation of animal life, and (3) the creation of man.

The phrase "In the beginning, God created" in verse 1:1 denotes the creation of the universe by the generation of the primeval fireball ("Let there be light") that marked the beginning of the physical universe (the big bang). This is the *only* act of *physical* creation (creation *ex nihilo*) that is mentioned in the entire first chapter.

The phrase "And God created the large sea-creatures" in verse 1:21 refers to the first animals.[2] The verb "created" in this context denotes the act of imparting life to inanimate matter, thereby changing it into something fundamentally different.

The phrase "And God created man" in verse 1:27 refers to contemporary Modern Man. The verb "created" in this context denotes endowing Modern Man with the unique intellectual and creative abilities that set him so completely apart from all other species in the animal kingdom. Man's mental gifts are so vastly superior to those of every other animal that they are *qualitatively* different. In that sense, man is a fundamentally different creature. His unique intellectual capabilities have enabled contemporary man to assume the dominant role on our planet.

Except for these three acts of creation, the biblical account of the development of the universe can be explained in terms of the present-day laws of nature. However, as of this writing, these three acts of creation have *no scientific explanation*.

CREDO

I feel compelled, as an observant Jew, to conclude this book by stating my views regarding the analysis presented here. As a professional scientist, I am impressed, indeed inspired, by the consistency that can be demonstrated between modern science and the Book of Genesis. Nevertheless, I want to emphasize that it is *not* for this reason that I am an observant Jew. I am observant because I have taken upon myself the commitment to fulfill the divine command as interpreted by traditional Jewish authorities. If I were to find that traditional Judaism appeared to be inconsistent with certain aspects of modern science, this would in no way weaken my commitment. I view questions as an incentive to further study—not as a cause for despair, and certainly not as a reason to reject my tradition. Indeed, it is the *absence* of questions that should give one cause for concern. In the study of the biblical text, as well as in scientific studies, a constantly searching attitude is an essential prerequisite for furthering one's understanding. Our Sages have emphasized that "he who hesitates to ask questions does not learn."[3]

NOTES

1. One may wonder why the three verses that deal with the seventh day—the Sabbath—were placed in the second chapter. Since the Sabbath marks the completion of the biblical account of the creation, one would expect these verses to be placed at the end of the first chapter. The interesting explanation is that these three verses *were* placed at the end of the first chapter—exactly where they belong—in the Jewish division of the Book of Genesis into chapters (see, for example, the Koren edition). The Catholic Vulgate, however, placed these three verses in the second chapter, and the chapter division of the Bible as found in the Vulgate has long been in virtually universal use; it is found in almost all present-day Hebrew texts and, of course, in English translations of the Bible, both Jewish and Christian.

2. The biblical text does not, of course, deal with microscopic bateria and protozoa that are not visible to the naked eye.

3. Mishnah, Avot 2:5.

APPENDIX A

Geological time scale, listing the eras and the periods.

Era	Period	Time (millions of years ago)
Cenozoic	Tertiary	
		65
Mesozoic	Cretaceous	
		135
	Jurassic	
		190
	Triassic	
		225
Paleozoic	Permian	
		280
	Carboniferous	
		345
	Devonian	
		395
	Silurian	
		430
	Ordovician	
		500
	Cambrian	
		570
	Precambrian	

APPENDIX B

Archaeological time scale, listing the cultural ages and the hominid species belonging to the genus *Homo*. The time scale has been expanded for recent times.

Cultural Age	Hominid Species	Time (thousands of years ago)
Neolithic		
		10
	Modern Man (*Homo sapiens sapiens*)	
		40
Paleolithic	Neanderthal Man (*Homo sapiens neanderthalensis*)	
		100
		300
	Homo erectus	
		1700 (?)
	Homo habilis	
		2000 (?)

APPENDIX C

Biographical notes about the Biblical commentators mentioned in the text.

MALBIM (1809–1879)
Rabbi Meir Loeb ben Yehiel Michael
Lived in several towns, primarily in Eastern Europe
Biblical commentator

ONKELOS (second century)
Lived in Roman Palestine
Wrote the definitive translation of the Bible into Aramaic

RADAK (1160–1235)
Rabbi David Kimche of Provence, Southern France
Biblical commentator and grammarian

RAMBAN (1194–1270)
Rabbi Moshe ben Nachman of Northern Spain
Talmudist and Biblical commentator

RASHI (1040–1105)
Rabbi Shlomo ben Isaac of Northern France
Most famous of the Biblical and Talmudic commentators

SAADIAH GAON (882–942)
Rabbi Saadiah ben Joseph of Egypt and Babylonia
Greatest of the later Babylonian scholars

SFORNO (c. 1470–1550)
Rabbi Ovadiah ben Jacob of Italy
Biblical commentator

INDEX OF BIBLICAL COMMENTATORS

INDEX OF SCIENTISTS

SUBJECT INDEX

Aviezer, Nathan.
In the beginning-- :
Biblical creation and
science